Series / Number 07-080

COMPUTER-ASSISTED INTERVIEWING

WILLEM E. SARIS
University of Amsterdam

SAGE PUBLICATIONS
The International Professional Publishers
Newbury Park   London   New Delhi

For information address:

SAGE Publications, Inc.
2455 Teller Road
Newbury Park, California 91320

SAGE Publications Ltd.
6 Bonhill Street
London EC2A 4PU
United Kingdom

SAGE Publications India Pvt. Ltd.
M-32 Market
Greater Kailash I
New Delhi 110 048 India

Printed in the United States of America

Saris, Willem E.
    Computer-assisted interviewing / Willem E. Saris.
        p. cm. — (Sage university papers series. Quantitative
    applications in the social sciences ; no. 80)
    Includes bibliographical references.
    ISBN 0-8039-4066-1
    1. Interviewing — Data processing. 2. Social surveys — Data
    processing. I. Title. II. Series.
    H61.28.S27 1991
    001.4'222—dc 20   91-22008

FIRST PRINTING, 1991

Sage Production Editor: Diane S. Foster

When citing a university paper, please use the proper form. Remember to cite the current Sage University Paper series title and include the paper number. One of the following formats can be adapted (depending on the style manual used):

(1) SARIS, W. E. (1991) Computer-Assisted Interviewing. Sage University Paper Series on Quantitative Applications in the Social Sciences, 07-080. Newbury Park, CA: Sage.
OR
(2) Saris, W. E. (1991). *Computer-Assisted Interviewing* (Sage University Paper series on Quantitative Applications in the Social Sciences, series no. 07-080). Newbury Park, CA: Sage.

CONTENTS

SERIES EDITOR'S INTRODUCTION

Computer-assisted interviewing is a central part of the current revolution in the measurement of public opinion. Since Gallup established its reputation in the 1930s, the unchallenged data-gathering strategy of scientific survey research had been face-to-face, paper-and-pencil interviews of respondents. However, in the 1980s, computer assisted telephone interviewing (CATI) began to replace the face-to-face methodology. Instead of sitting in the respondent's living room, the interviewer now sat in an office behind a terminal, asked questions over the telephone, and entered the responses into a computer. In the United States today, most national surveys are conducted with some version of CATI rather than with face-to-face interviews.

In this well-organized monograph, Professor Saris explains CATI, along with many other kinds of computer-assisted data collection (CADAC). For example, in Chapter 2 he discusses computer-assisted personal interviews (CAPI), computerized self-administered questionnaires (CSAQ), computer-assisted panel research (CAPAR), and touchtone data entry (TDE). Some advocates of computer-assisted interviewing are quick to claim that it is faster and less expensive than traditional methods. However, Saris is more cautious on those points, emphasizing instead the potential gains in data quality. For instance, data cleaning can be done while the interviewee is still available, order effects from question placement and response categories can be overcome through randomization, interviewer performance can be monitored more easily, and wild code checks can occur immediately.

Nevertheless, computer-assisted interviewing is not without difficulty. A major concern is questionnaire design, to which Saris devotes an entire chapter (Chapter 3). Another important issue is the choice to be made from the "jungle" of computer programs available. In Chapter 4, hardware and software choices for CADAC are carefully discussed.

Although relatively new, computer-assisted interviewing offers the prospect of solving certain nagging problems resulting from traditional survey research methods. Take, as an illustration, how it can overcome the low-wave, high-attrition problems typical of panel studies. Saris helped create the

1

"tele-interview" system, whereby a random sample of Dutch households regularly is interviewed on home personal computers, and their answers automatically returned to a central computer. With such a system in place, the panel researcher readily could conduct repeated waves and expect little drop-out from respondents. This, and many other innovative examples of CADAC, are considered by Saris in this excellent volume.

—*Michael S. Lewis-Beck*
Series Editor

ACKNOWLEDGMENTS

I would like to thank my Ph.D. students for their important contributions to this book in the form of our continuous discussions. I also thank my colleagues Mike Lewis-Beck, Robert Groves, Dirk Sikkel, Mick Couper, Carol House, and Harm Hartman, and two anonymous reviewers for their critical comments on the text.

PREFACE

Anyone who has been involved in survey research is aware that it requires a lot of people, effort, and money. Questionnaires must be designed, typed, printed, distributed by mail, filled in, returned, coded, entered into the computer, and validated. Only after all these steps have been taken can the analysis start.

The use of the computer in data collection can considerably reduce the amount of work. In computer-assisted data collection (CADAC), an interview program presents the questions on the screen and registers the answers, which are immediately entered into the computer. In this way one can skip the printing, mailing, coding, and data entry. If extra attention is paid to the construction of the interview, even the validation or editing phase can be reduced considerably. This reduction of work would suggest that computer-assisted data collection has the advantage of being faster and cheaper. Nicholls and Groves (1986), however, have mentioned that there is very little evidence for this general conclusion.

There is also another reason why CADAC has been recommended by many researchers. Nicholls (1978), Groves (1983), Fink (1983), Dekker and Dorn (1984), and many others have claimed that CADAC will lead to improvements in the data quality in survey and panel research. They have in mind data quality improvement by automatic branching and coding, consistency checks, and many other possibilities. There is very little empirical evidence (Groves and Nicholls, 1986), however, to suggest that these claims are justified.

Nevertheless, the use of CADAC is growing each year. It started in the 1970s with computer-assisted telephone interviewing (CATI), which is now widely used in commercial research, at universities, and by government agencies (Nicholls and Groves, 1986; Spaeth, 1990). The total number of CATI installations is unknown, but is probably more than 1,000 over the whole world (Gonzalez, 1990). In 1988, the U.S. government alone already had more than 50 installations. The National Agricultural Statistical Service of the United States now is doing more than 125,000 CATI interviews each year.

More recently, computer-assisted personal interviewing (CAPI) has been introduced. Government agencies in the U.S. and Europe (Thornberry, Rowe, and Bigger, 1990; van Bastelaer, Kerssemakers, and Sikkel, 1988) and marketing research firms in Europe are among those using these facilities for data collection. In the Netherlands, the use of CAPI procedures by the Dutch Statistical Office alone has grown very rapidly, from nearly zero 5 years ago to more than 3,000 uses per month in 1990.

All large commercial firms now have CAPI facilities as well. A similar trend can be seen in most of the Western European countries and in the United States. There also have been experiments and commercial applications using computer-assisted interviewing procedures, in which no interviewers are used. All of them are designed for panel surveys. Some use videotex systems (Clemens, 1984); others use home computers (de Pijper and Saris, 1986a) or existing computer networks (Gonzalez, 1990; Kiesler and Sproull, 1986). There also have been experiments with the use of touchtone telephones (Clayton and Harrel, 1989) and voice recognition (Winter and Clayton, 1990). The last two procedures are used mainly on a small scale for obtaining business information. With the home-computer-based system, called *tele-interviewing*, 150,000 interviews per year are performed in the Netherlands.

This continuing growth of CADAC suggests that at least one of the three arguments should hold: increased speed, reduction in costs, or improvement in data quality. It is quite likely that all three arguments hold for different projects. On the one hand, simple research can be done very quickly and cheaply using CADAC if one is not trying to improve the data quality. On the other hand, complex research can be done better than before using the new tools of CADAC, but probably will not be cheaper or faster.

Many different topics would be interesting enough for discussion in this monograph. For example, we could discuss the following:

- The cost-effectiveness of the extra equipment and extra employees needed to maintain the computer systems
- The extra skills required of interviewers and respondents, and the consequences for training time and/or nonresponse
- The increased and decreased flexibility of the process
- The consequences of the introduction of CADAC systems for research organization

In this monograph, however, we do not want to discuss these topics. Instead, we want to concentrate on the improvement of data quality as the central issue. We have chosen this aspect because it is of concern to all social scientists who are collecting data. It already is possible to improve the quality of data using CADAC. One clear example of this is given by Tortora (1985), who has shown that 77% of the data errors in a standard survey, which were so serious they normally would require a second contact with the respondents, could be avoided by the use of CADAC with on-line edit facilities (allowing the program to check for inconsistencies and ask for corrections during the interview). This advantage, however, is not obtained for free: more must be done than "only" writing a questionnaire. To this task, the researcher must add the following (House and Nicholls, 1988):

- Branching and skipping instructions
- Specified "fills"
- On-line range and consistency checks
- Help screens
- Types of answers to the questions
- The way the answers must be registered

Some more tools will be added to this list of basic procedures in order to increase the possibilities. But one thing is clear: Computer-assisted interviewing requires not only the skill of writing normal questionnaires as taught in many books (e.g., Converse and Presser, 1986; Sudman and Bradburn, 1974), but also new skills related to the new possibilities. The purpose of this monograph is to give the reader an idea of these possibilities and the difficulties that will arise if one ventures down the road of computer-assisted interviewing.

We start in Chapter 1 with a general introduction to computer-assisted interviewing. In Chapter 2, we discuss the extra possibilities that computer-assisted interviewing has to offer to interviewer-administered interviewing, self-administered interviewing, and panel surveys. In Chapter 3, we discuss the design of questionnaires for CADAC. In Chapter 4, we give a brief overview of important features of programs for computer-assisted interviewing that must be considered if one wants to purchase a CADAC program.

A number of examples of questionnaires from research are given. These examples are not limited to a specific interview program. We concentrate on the logical structure rather than on the language used. In this monograph, examples are presented as annotated versions of normal questionnaires (Baker and Lefes, 1988). In such questionnaires, their relation to the usual paper questionnaires remains visible, and the extra statements needed for computer-assisted interviewing become very clear. There are programs that use quite different procedures, as we discuss later, but for my purposes the procedure used here is sufficient to illustrate the task of the interview designer.

COMPUTER-ASSISTED INTERVIEWING

WILLEM E. SARIS
University of Amsterdam

1. COMPUTER-ASSISTED INTERVIEWING

Personal and telephone interviews consist of a specific type of dialogue between an interviewer and a respondent. In such a dialogue, the task of the interviewer is rather complex. She or he must do the following.

- Obtain cooperation
- Present information, questions, answer categories, and instructions
- Motivate the respondent to answer
- Build up sufficient confidentiality for honest answers to be given
- Stop the respondent from recounting irrelevant stories
- Check if the answers are appropriate
- Help the respondent if the question is not correctly understood
- Code the answers in prespecified categories, or write the answers down
- Look for the next question

Compared with the task of the interviewer, the respondent has a simpler task. He or she must only do the following.

- Interpret the question
- Examine his or her memory (or papers) for the information
- Answer the question orally or write it down
- Possibly code the answer using a specific code book

Given the list of tasks the interviewer must perform in an interview, one might wonder whether anyone can perform all of them in one interview. Surprisingly, the process normally leads to satisfactory results. That does not mean that the interview has not been criticized in the past. Some critics have shown that respondents provide biased answers as a result of misunderstanding the questions (Belson, 1981; Molenaar, 1986; Schuman and Presser,

1981), social desirability (Bradburn, Sudman, Blair, and Stocking, 1978; Kalton and Schuman, 1982; Phillips and Clancy, 1970), or response set (Converse and Presser, 1986; Schuman and Presser, 1981). Others have concentrated on the problems of interviewer effects (e.g., Dijkstra and van der Zouwen, 1982; Groves, 1989). Bruinsma, Saris, and Gallhofer (1980), Andrews (1984), van Doorn, Saris, and Lodge (1983), and Saris (1988) have shown that the choice of response scale has a considerable effect on the results of a study. There also has been a lot of discussion in the literature about failure to recall information (Sikkel, 1985; Sudman and Bradburn, 1973, 1974) in interviews that ask questions about past behavior. Such studies, which often use diaries, are notorious for their high nonresponse (Thornton, Freedman, and Camburn, 1982), mainly due to the amount of effort asked of the respondent. Recently, there has been an increasing tendency to use electronic equipment instead of diaries. Modern techniques allow the registration of some kinds of behavior, such as watching TV, using the telephone, buying consumer goods, and so on, without putting any questions to the subjects. Such systems can be seen as a promising effort to design unobtrusive measurement instruments (Webb, Campbell, Schwartz, and Sechrest, 1981) that could replace the notoriously unreliable diaries. (See Saris, 1989, for an overview article on this development.) If these procedures turn out to be efficient, they will certainly lead to a complete change in data collection with respect to behavioral data. However, this monograph does not deal with that development, but instead concentrates on data collection by questionnaires.

Besides the above-mentioned methodological problems, there is a practical problem with interviews: namely, the costs of interviewing. In the United States, the costs of face-to-face interviewing are already so high that most research is done by telephone or mail.

Other problems are nonresponse in the form of complete refusals, especially in large cities, and partial nonresponse as a consequence of complex routings in the questionnaires.

The recently developed computer-based procedures for data collection can solve at least some of these problems. Below, we will discuss in historical order computer-assisted interviewing procedures that are efficiently replacing the paper-and-pencil procedures of the past, but first, we consider the requirements for an interview program if it is to replace a paper questionnaire or an interviewer.

CADAC as a Substitute for Paper Questionnaires

At a minimum, an interview program should be able to replace a paper questionnaire. A more ambitious goal would be for the program to replace the interviewer, or at least to reduce the task of the interviewer to minimal proportions. One could imagine the computer program doing all the administrative work, which it can do better than the interviewer, leaving for the interviewer the task of motivating and explaining, which the interviewer probably can do better than the computer.

The requirements for an interview program to replace a paper questionnaire are as follows.

- The presentation of information, questions, answer categories, and instructions
- The registration of the answers etc.
- Branching to the next question

These requirements are minimal and all interview programs can perform these tasks. Nevertheless, they are more complex than they may appear. One reason is that any type of question must be possible, and the computer should know the type of response (i.e., numeric or alphanumeric) and the size of the response. In order to present a question on a screen, the interview program must have the following information (Nicholls and House, 1987).

- What type of question is asked
- What the size of the answer is
- Where the data must be stored
- Where the text starts
- Where the text ends

Any interview program must deal with these tasks and each of them does it in a different way. Some programs provide a computer programming language, and are therefore very flexible but difficult to use; others are interpreters and try to stay as close as possible to the form of normal interviews (de Bie, Stoop, and de Vries, 1989). Some are question-based, and others are screen- or form-based (Nicholls, 1988). No matter what program is used, some extra information must always be provided, as we have indicated above. In these examples, we use a language derived from the program INTERV (de Pijper and Saris, 1986b), because by using that program (an interpreter) it becomes very clear what part of the questionnaire is added to instruct the computer.

Type = Num range=[10   120] var=Age
How old are you ?
(type the answer below)
END

Figure 1.1. Example 1

Let us see how a normal question can be formulated for an interview program. As an example, take the question, "How old are you?" In order to specify the task for an interview program to present this question on the screen, the instruction must be written like the one presented in Example 1 (Figure 1.1). A program requires that the lines containing instructions to the computer are distinguished from the lines of text that should appear on the screens. Therefore, all instructions to the program are printed in bold letters, and screen text is printed in plain letters in all figures.

The following information is indicated in the first line of Example 1 (Figure 1.1): the type of question (numeric), the acceptable range of answers (10 to 120), and where the question must be stored (in the variable *age*). After this instruction line, the question itself follows with the instruction to the respondent. Because these lines are not in bold, the program automatically assumes that these lines are to be presented on the screen. The researcher has complete control over the layout of the screens by placing the text wherever she or he wants. The interview screen will look exactly as specified. The text is followed by a last instruction. This line is necessary to indicate where the text of the screen stops. Normally, the specification of the next instruction is automatically the end of the previous one. If there is no next question, the end of the questionnaire is indicated by "END."

If this small interview were tried on a computer, the result should be as indicated in Figure 1.2. This example demonstrates how the program interprets the instructions and presents on the screen exactly what has been written down for the screen text.

If the interviewer types in the answer (for example, "25") this number is automatically stored in the variable *age* and can be used at any moment later in the interview.

In this simple example with only one question there is no need to indicate where to go after the first question. Example 2 (Figure 1.3) is an illustration of a longer questionnaire, with several different questions and indications for branching.

```
┌─────────────────────────────────┐
│  How old are you ?              │
│  (type the answer below)        │
│                                 │
│                                 │
└─────────────────────────────────┘
```

Figure 1.2. Screen of Example 1

This more realistic example demonstrates more clearly the different characteristics that an interview program should have if it is to be used for the presentation of questions during an interview. These basic characteristics are as follows.

- Instructions and screens should be distinguished (bold or not)
- The type of response should be indicated (by type=)
- The size of the response should be indicated (by a range= [a b])
- The registration of answers should be organized (in the data file and in variables)
- The beginning and end of a screen should be indicated
- The branching should be indicated (condition)

Example 2 (Figure 1.3) shows how these different requirements are satisfied for the program used here. The interview starts with an information screen, and, therefore, the first instruction is **Information** so the program does not expect an answer. After the information screen, it is indicated that seven questions will be asked. Several types of questions are possible. Here are illustrated questions that require numeric answers (type=num), self-made category scales (type=cat), a prestructured 5-point rating scale (type=rating), a time scale (type=time), and an open question (type=open). A program can provide many more types. For example, the program INTERV has 16 different types of questions, including line-production scales, prestructured-category scales, multiple-answer scales, money scales, and an automatic-coding scale.

Branching is done automatically by the computer program. The branching can be arranged in different ways. Branching is indicated here by conditional statements (lines starting with the instruction **Condition**). This is very similar to how instructions to interviewers commonly are done (e.g., "Only for people with work"). In this case, these instructions are interpreted by the program, which presents only the appropriate questions to the interviewer

14

Information
In this interview, we would like to
ask you about your activities.
# of Questions=7
Type=cat range= [0   1] var=work
Do you have a job ?
  0 No
  1 Yes
Type=open var=job
Condition Work=1
  What is your occupation ?
  (describe the occupation as fully as possible)
Type=num range=[0   20] var=hours
Condition Work=1
  How many hours did you work yesterday ?
Type=time var=time
Condition Work=1
  At what time did you start your work ?
Type=cat range =[1   6] var=other
Condition Work=0
  What is your situation ?
  1 housewife
  2 pensioner
  3 student
  4 unemployed
  5 disabled
  6 other
Type=code var=act
Condition Work=0
  What was your main activity yesterday ?
Type=rating text=var
  Did you enjoy your day or not yesterday ?
  terrible   very pleasant
  day   day
END

Figure 1.3. Example 2

or respondent depending on the answers given. Other procedures will be discussed later. The resulting screens for Example 2 are shown in Figure 1.4.

Figure 1.4 shows that there are two routes specified to this questionnaire. The route chosen depends on the response to the question "Do you have a job?" and thus the value of the variable *work*.

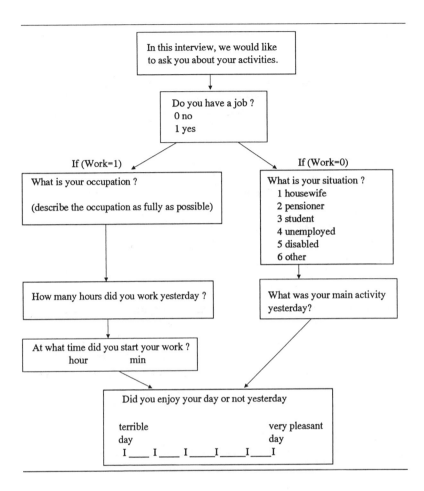

Figure 1.4. Screens of Example 2

This extended example illustrates that it is not too difficult to write questionnaires for interview programs that can replace paper questionnaires; in fact, the difference between the two is not so large. The computer questionnaire simply requires a few more instructions for the computer.

CADAC as a Partial Substitute for Interviewers

Let us now look at the requirements for an interview program to replace completely the paper questionnaire *and* interviewer. In this case, there are a number of extra requirements. Looking again at the list of tasks required of the interviewer, the following tasks have not yet been fulfilled by the interview program.

- Obtain cooperation
- Motivate the respondent to answer
- Build up sufficient confidentiality for honest answers to be given
- Stop the respondent from recounting irrelevant stories
- Check if the answers are appropriate
- Help the respondent if the question is not correctly understood
- Code the answers in predetermined categories
- Write the answer down

It is clear that an interview program cannot perform the social tasks as well as the interviewer. This, however, does not necessarily mean that the programs are worse on all counts. For example, respondents do not tell irrelevant stories to computers, and they are often more willing to report undesirable behavior to a computer than to an interviewer. However, here we concentrate on those technical tasks that can be performed as well or even better by the computer than by the interviewer. These tasks are as follows.

- Check if the answers are appropriate
- Help the respondent if the question is not correctly understood
- Code the answers in predetermined categories
- Write the answer down

The interviewer has only very limited possibilities for checking the correctness of the answers (range checks). A computer program not only can carry out range checks, but also can check the answer against any kind of existing knowledge that may validate or invalidate the answer.

The interviewer can certainly help people if necessary, but if a research project is well designed, one can build help options into an interview program as well.

Coding during an interview is a very time-consuming and difficult task for the interviewer. While concentrating on the coding, she or he also must keep up the contact with the respondents, which can lead to problems. Two computer procedures that can be substituted for coding by the interviewer or respondent are shown below.

Finally, it is not difficult to provide a simple editor that allows people to write short remarks. Experience shows that the respondents are very reluctant to do so in the beginning, but after some experience they like it and even ask for it.

Example 3 (Figure 1.5) illustrates how these possibilities can be realized using an interview program. The example is a typical marketing research questionnaire about cigarette smoking. The questionnaire starts with a general question, but it quickly becomes clear that the researcher is only interested in the type and brand of cigarettes the respondent may have bought. The line in the questionnaire is easy to follow by looking at the questions. If one also takes into account the branching, it is even clearer. In this case, for each categorical answer to a question, the instructions indicate in sequence which question should be asked next. For example, if the answer to the first question is "yes," the next question is "what?" whereas if the answer is "no," the next question is "end." This means that the program jumps to the end of the questionnaire. Therefore the routing indicates that only respondents who bought something to smoke should answer further questions. These respondents are asked to characterize in three questions the type of smoking articles they bought. On the basis of the category values used, the interview can distinguish seven types of smokers from the three questions of the "tree" type:

1	cigars
211	cigarettes, filter, low tar
212	cigarettes, filter, high tar
221	cigarettes, no filter, low tar
222	cigarettes, no filter, high tar
3	cigarette-rolling tobacco
4	pipe tobacco

The tree-type questions automatically produce the above specified codes on the basis of the category codes of the different questions. For example, if one bought cigars, a "1" is coded on the first question and nothing more. If one bought low-tar, filter cigarettes, the answers on the tree questions are, respectively, 2, 1, and 1, and the code is 211. This has been called *tree-structured coding*, because it is a procedure by which the

Information

In this interview, we would like to
ask you about your shopping.

# of questions=7

Type=cat range=[1   2] var=shop

Did you buy anything to smoke yesterday ?

1 yes − − − − → **what**

2 no − − − − → **end**

Type=tree range=[1   4] var=what

What did you buy ?

1 cigars   − − − − − − → **end**

2 cigarettes   − − − − − → **filt**

3 cigarette-rolling tobacco − − − − − − → **end**

4 pipe tobacco   − − − − − − → **end**

Type=tree range=[1   2] var=filt

Did they have a filter or not ?

1 filter

2 without filter

Type=tree range= [1   2] var=tar

Was it a high-or low-tar cigarette ?

1 low

2 high

Type=code var=brand

What brand of cigarettes did you buy ?

Codes: 1 "pall mal" "pal mal " "pal mall" "pall mall"

2 "marboro" "mar_" "marlboro"

3 "lucky_" "_ strike" "lucky strike"

4 "camal" "cammel" "camell" "camel"

Type=price range=[0   2000] var=costs

How much did you pay ?

Type=price Help var=corr

Condition (costs > 300 or costs < 200)

Help screen

Most packs of cigarettes cost between
200 and 300 cents.

Question Screen

The price you mentioned is very unlikely.
For further information press F3.
If you made a mistake press F1.
If the answer was correct specify the reasons
below. You can use the rest of this
screen for your comments.

End

Figure 1.5. Example 3

interviewer or the respondent can code products or activities by answering simple tree-structured questions.

Of course, this is a very simple example, but the same has been done for the coding of occupations (150 different categories) and companies (100 categories) for labor-force surveys, activities (350 different categories) for time-budget research (Verweij, Kalfs, and Saris, 1986), and consumer products (3,000 different categories) for consumer expenditure surveys (Hartman and Saris, 1991). This procedure avoids the need for an elaborate code book to be used by the respondent (or interviewer or coder). It is hypothesized that this reduction of effort will lead to more precise and valid results, but there has not yet been any detailed research on this point.

In the third part of the interview in Example 3 (Figure 1.5), the brand of the product is asked for in an open question. The codes that have been mentioned after the questions are the categories of the code book that are used for "string matching" in order to classify the answers. These codes are not presented on the respondent's screen. Because many different errors can be expected in the writing of the respondents, the code book is made in such a way that it allows the respondents to make errors. This can be done in two ways. First of all, all expected errors can be specified (see Pall Mall and Camel). Secondly, one can ask the computer to match only a characteristic part of the word; the rest is indicated by a line (see Marlboro and Lucky Strike).

Both coding procedures, by tree-structured questions and string matching, serve one purpose, the classification of answers to questions that normally need coding, without putting the full burden of the coding on the respondents or interviewers. Which of the two procedures is used depends on the topic and the taste of the researcher, but one should be warned that both procedures require a lot of research in advance.

The last two questions of Example 3 (Figure 1.5) illustrate the help, checking, and writing possibilities of interview programs. The first question asks for the price. The second question starts by instructing the program that it is an open question, that there is a help screen, and gives the name of the question (var=corr), after which a check on the range of the answer to the previous question is specified. If the answer to the previous question is outside the expected range, the last question is asked. In this question, help is provided on a screen and this can be requested by pressing "F3." In this case, the question consists of two parts, a help screen and a question screen. The program should be told that there are two screens, so the help is mentioned in the instruction line. Of course, this grammar is program specific, but a similar facility has been created in most advanced programs.

This question suggests that the last answer might be wrong; further information is given on the help screen, and the previous question can be corrected by pressing "F1," which will present the previous question again. It is also possible that the answer is correct, but that (for example) more than one pack of cigarettes was purchased. This answer can be given on the rest of the screen by writing a remark down. Of course, the editor provided should be very simple so people can handle it without help. In INTERV, the editor allows writing without returns at the end of the line (word wrap) and corrections can be made using the backspace key, but no other possibilities are provided.

Now that we have discussed the questionnaire as it is specified in this particular case, I will illustrate the sequence of screens that result from this questionnaire (Figure 1.6). Because the reader probably knows by now what the screens look like, we only illustrate the structure of the interview with a flow chart indicating the names of the screens and variables.

This example illustrates that writing a questionnaire that takes over certain tasks of the interviewer is not very complicated. We illustrated procedures for automatic branching, two automatic coding procedures, help options, checks, and possibilities for open-ended questions. In the next section, we hope to show that there are several tasks that the computer can do even better than the interviewer.

CADAC Can Be Better Than Normal Interviewing

Although we would not say that interview programs are better than interviewers in all aspects of the task, there certainly are a number of aspects in which the interview programs are better. Let us look at the following technical skills.

- Calculations
- Substitutions of previous answers
- Randomization of questions and answer categories
- Validation of responses
- Complex branching
- Complex coding
- Exact formulation of questions and information
- Provision of comparable help

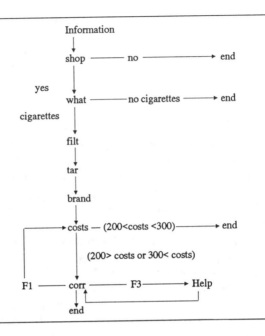

Figure 1.6. Flow Chart for Example 3

In the case of the last two skills, the advantage of using an interview program is obvious. It is well known (Brenner, 1982; Dijkstra, 1983) that interviewers do not read the questions exactly as they have been formulated. Also, help, when needed, does not always take the same form. As a consequence, it is unclear whether the responses to the questions are comparable. In computer-assisted interviewing where self-administration is used, this problem no longer exists, because the interviewer does not read the questions and therefore the questions on the screen are the same for all respondents.

The discussion of complex coding and routing also can be kept very brief, as these possibilities have already been discussed in the previous section. The only further remark needed is that the possibilities an interviewer has during an interview with respect to coding and branching are very limited, as the interviewer's task is already difficult enough. It is impractical to take longer than 30 seconds between questions to determine the code or the routing. For complex coding or branching more time is needed, and the interviewer will have trouble with the different tasks that must be performed. For a computer, such tasks are no problem; it can easily determine a routing on the basis of the answers to 10 or more questions within a second, and the complex codings also can be performed very quickly. String matching with 256 categories does not lead to a noticeable time delay in INTERV. Given these qualities of the interview programs, it is better to assign these tasks to an interview program than to an interviewer. Let us now turn to an example that illustrates the possibilities of programs with respect to calculation, substitution, and branching.

It is clear that one cannot ask an interviewer to make calculations during the interview. Nevertheless, sometimes it is useful to make calculations to determine the branching to the next question or to substitute the result of the calculations in the text of the interview. Example 4 (Figure 1.7) illustrates this point in a simple questionnaire that is nevertheless too complex for interviewers.

This example again concerns the purchase of cigarettes, using two questions from the previous example. The new aspect in this example is that a more complex situation is discussed. The possibility that more than one pack of cigarettes could have been purchased is explicitly taken into account. We expect the price of a pack of cigarettes to be between 200 and 300 cents, and so the lower and upper bound of the price paid for cigarettes are, respectively, "number * 200" and "number * 300," where "number" is the number of packs bought. A computer can calculate these costs simply, but it would be too much for an interviewer to do calculations like this in the course of an interview. The computer also can calculate how many packs most likely have been bought, assuming that the total amount paid is correct. This number is estimated to be "costs divided by 250." If all these numbers have been calculated, more detailed help can be given to the respondents during the interview. Example 4 (Figure 1.7) shows that after the two basic questions, calculations are made (grouped in what is called a *calculation block*). The calculated values of the variables then are used in the condition for the next question and the help screen. This is done by substituting these numbers for different variables in the text (for this purpose quotation marks are used before the variable to be substituted). Clearly, this information cannot be provided by interviewers, who do not have time to make such calculations. In computer-assisted interviews, such calculations do not cause any delay.

This example illustrates the extra possibilities offered by computer-assisted interviewing as a result of the facility to make calculations. Calculations

---

# of Questions=2
Type=num range=[0   25] var=number
   How many packs of cigarettes did you buy yesterday ?
type=price range=[100   1000] var=costs
   How much did you pay for the cigarettes ?
Calculations
V2= number*200
V3= number*300
V4=costs/250
# of Questions=1
type=price Help var=corr
Condition ((costs > v2) Or (costs > v3))
Help Screen
   Most packs of cigarettes cost between 200 and 300 cents.
   Thus the costs for "number packs would be between "number*200="v2
   and "number * 300="v3.
   The price you mentioned of "costs is very unlikely. It would mean that you have bought
   approximately "costs/250="V4 packs of cigarettes and not "V1 as you mentioned.
Question screen
   The price you mentioned is very unlikely.
   For further information press F3.
   If your answer was correct type 0.
   If you made a mistake specify the proper costs :
END

Figure 1.7. Example 4

can play an important role in substitution and branching, which can be considerably more complex in computer-assisted interviewing than in paper-and-pencil interviews.

Example 4 (Figure 1.7) also illustrates another, very important, new feature of computer-assisted interviewing, the improved facilities for validation. Normally, the interviewers do not have the time or skill to carry out the validation during the interview. In computer-assisted interviewing, validation can be done immediately. As soon as the answer to a question is given, it can be checked against other information to check the quality of the answer. In case of doubt, the program can immediately ask the respondent for clarification and corrections (see Figure 1.7). This is a very important advantage of computer-assisted interviewing. It means that one can clean the data while the respondent is still available. Normally, these checks are done later, and if errors are detected, one can only change the incorrect answer into a missing value to avoid returning to the respondents for additional information. In computer-assisted interviewing, these checks are made during the interview, and if the questionnaire is constructed with care, the data from the research can be considered optimal immediately after the interview is finished; later validation will not be necessary. We will illustrate this point elsewhere in this monograph, as it is one of the most important advantages of computer-assisted interviewing.

The last two points to be mentioned in this section are randomization of questions and randomization of response categories. Because of the "order effect" in interviews (Billiet, Loosveldt, and Waterplas, 1984; Schuman and Presser, 1981), it has been suggested that the sequence of questions and response categories be randomized. In normal paper-and-pencil interviews this is not very easy. It requires different versions of the questionnaire, which is very costly, and only a few variants can be created.

In CADAC, randomization can be realized in a simple way, because a random-number generator can easily be created and used during the interview to determine the order of the questions. The researcher must decide only in which way to tell the program which questions have to be randomized. This requires a statement specifying the names of the questions to be randomized. If the questions already are brought together in a block (as in a stimulus block; see de Pijper and Saris, 1986b), the questions can be randomized by default, or only one sign has to be used to specify that randomization is requested. The same holds for category randomization, but in that case the categories already belong together, and only a sign in the instructions for the program is necessary.

Disadvantages of CADAC

There are also some disadvantages associated with CADAC. Groves and Nicholls (1986) mention the following points.

- The size of the screen is smaller than a questionnaire page, which might lead to a lack of overview when using CADAC
- Corrections are more easily made on a form
- Coordination of hand and eye is lost

Because a screen is smaller than a questionnaire page, a screen cannot contain as much information. In the earlier CADAC programs, each question was presented on a separate screen in order to have enough space for the questions. The disadvantage of this approach is that people can lose track of the purpose of the questions, especially if automatic branching is used extensively. The problem has been recognized in the literature and has been referred to as the "segmentation" problem (House and Nicholls, 1988). One solution to this problem is to use programs that present more questions on one screen (Nicholls, 1988). Another solution is to use screens that summarize information. We will return to these options later.

The second problem is that paper questionnaires give a continuous overview of the questions and answers, so that one can easily see where errors have been made and correct them. In a computer-assisted procedure these corrections are not so easily made if an "item-based" program is used. The CADAC user must return to the error in the questionnaire by moving backwards through the questionnaire, or the researcher must provide correction possibilities at any place where problems can occur. The first option might lead to errors if the program or questionnaire is not protected against such errors (Nicholls and House, 1987). The second option requires a lot of effort on the part of the researcher.

The last problem—the lack of coordination of hand and eye in CADAC— is a very interesting problem. In paper questionnaires, people write where they look. In CADAC procedures, people type on a keyboard, but they have to look at a screen for the result. If they look at their fingers and not at the screen while they are typing, there is a possibility of making an error in the response. Such an error is very unlikely in paper questionnaires. Although this problem has not been very closely studied, it is probably the experience of many users of CADAC systems that typing errors do occur in CADAC procedures and that they can have a negative influence on the data quality. The solution to this problem is to use summary screens, which we will discuss later.

All three problems indicate that CADAC procedures are not the same as paper-and-pencil interviews. Simple translations of paper-and-pencil interviews to computer-assisted procedures will not necessarily lead to better quality data. More effort in the design is required in order to make the CADAC questionnaires better than paper-and-pencil questionnaires. Facilities that can be used for this purpose are the topic of Chapter 2, but first, let us summarize the results so far.

Summary

We have shown in this chapter that interview programs combined with good questionnaires not only can replace paper questionnaires, but also can replace the interviewer, at least partially. We also have demonstrated that computer-assisted interviewing can even be superior to personal interviewing, because of the possibility of calculations, complex fills, complex branching, coding, randomization of questions and answers, and, most important, the possibility of validating the answers during the interview while the respondent is still present. During the interviews, checks can be done and the respondents can introduce the necessary corrections or can indicate why their case is different from the normal case.

On the other hand, we also have mentioned that there are some problems with CADAC procedures that require extra attention. Therefore, it should be clear that there is a price to pay for improving data quality with the use of CADAC. The price is not the cost of the computer itself, which is quickly covered as a result of the efficiency of the procedures. The higher costs result from the time one must spend on the development of good questionnaires that take full advantage of the facilities of computer-assisted interviewing to improve the data quality. Such a time investment makes more sense for questionnaires that are very frequently used.

Because the procedures for improving the data quality differ according to the data-collection techniques used, we will discuss the possibilities of each of the different data-collection techniques in Chapter 2.

2. DIFFERENT CADAC APPLICATIONS

Having dealt with the general possibilities and difficulties of computer-assisted interviewing in Chapter 1, this chapter now discusses different possible applications of these techniques and their potential.

The oldest application of CADAC is computer-assisted telephone interviewing (CATI). Commercial applications of CATI began in the 1970s (Fink, 1983), and it is now widely used in commercial research, at universities, and by government agencies (Nicholls and Groves, 1986). The most recent figures for the universities given by Spaeth (1990) show that 69% of those university research institutions in the United States who replied to a questionnaire were using a CATI system, and that 22% more were planning to start CATI applications in the near future.

The first systems used as hardware were mainframes or minicomputers with connected terminals. Examples of such systems still existing are the Cases system (See Appendix) in the United States, and the Research Machine (Pulse Train Technology, 1984) in Europe. In recent years, more and more personal-computer- (PC-) based systems, stand-alones, and networked systems have become available (Carpenter, 1988).

Typical of all CATI systems is that the interviewer sits behind the terminal or PC and calls a respondent. Once contact is made, all necessary information and questions appear on the screen and the interviewer immediately types in the answers on the keyboard of the computer or terminal. This description shows that as far as the respondent is concerned, there is no difference between a CATI interview and a paper-and-pencil telephone interview. The difference for the interviewer is that part of the work is done by the computer (branching and skipping, fills, consistency checks, etc.). This is partially an advantage, but there are also disadvantages associated with this approach if the questionnaire is not well designed. The extra facilities offered by CATI systems are sample management by the CATI system, call management by the CATI system, and on-line monitoring of the interviewers.

The first two facilities will not be discussed further here, because they affect the quality of the sample rather than the quality of the responses. For further information on these points, see Nicholls and Groves (1986) and Weeks (1988), and other articles referenced in those texts. The third facility offered by CATI will be given some attention below.

The second CADAC system to be developed and tested was the computer-assisted personal interview (CAPI). As far as we are aware, the first tests were carried out in 1980. Although at that time computers still were not really practical for this purpose, a Dutch research group was experimenting with these procedures using Apple IIc computers and, later, transportable Kaypro computers, in order to test the possibilities of more efficient measurement procedures for attitudes, evaluations, and preferences (Saris, de Pijper, and Neijens, 1982). The first experiments with portable computers by a statistical office were reported by the Swedish Census Bureau (Danielsson and Maarstad, 1982). More recently, the Dutch Statistical Office has done several experiments (Bemelmans-Spork and Sikkel, 1985, 1986). Similar reports are now coming out of the United States (e.g., Couper and Groves, 1989; Couper, Groves, and Jacobs, 1989; Thornberry et al., 1990).

Since 1980, portable computers, or "laptops," have become much cheaper, lighter, and better. Therefore, it comes as no surprise that several statistical offices have decided to do at least a large part of their routine face-to-face interviewing with CAPI systems. As far as we are aware, this decision has been made in the Netherlands, Sweden, the United Kingdom, and the United States. Commercial firms also have started to use CAPI systems recently (Boerema, Baden, and Bon, 1987).

In CAPI, the interviewer takes the computer to the respondent's residence. Normally, the computer is used in the same way as in CATI applications: The questions appear on the screen, and the interviewer reads the questions for the respondents and types the answers into the computer. However, from the very start there has been another way of working, in which the interviewer leaves the reading of the questions and the entering of the answers completely to the respondent. This is sometimes called a "computerized self-administered questionnaire," or CSAQ.

From a respondent's point of view, the interviewer-administered CAPI interview is not very different from the paper-and-pencil interview, although it has been suggested that the mere presence of the computer might change the situation (Couper and Groves, 1989). The studies of the Dutch statistical office (Bemelmans-Spork and Sikkel, 1985), however, do not indicate any difference with respect to refusals or partial nonresponse, even for sensitive questions such as income. Nevertheless, there are differences: The CAPI interviews take longer than paper-and-pencil interviews, and the notes made by the interviewer on the computer are shorter (Couper and Groves, 1989).

Whatever the conclusion on this point in the future, may be it is safe to say that the interview situation changes quite dramatically in the self-administered approach. A much more active role is required of the respondent, as well as more skills than in interviewer-administered interviewing. (The latter does not apply if the program is sufficiently user friendly.) Saris et al. (1982), who used this approach in the Netherlands, did not report any problems, nor did Gavrilov (1988), even though his study was done with farmers in the Soviet Union who had very limited schooling.

Another important difference between the two CAPI systems is that in the self-administered procedure, the interviewer no longer has anything to do during the interview. It is for this reason that alternatives have been developed. One possibility is to create a situation where one researcher can help a number of respondents at the same time. For example, this can be done by placing a number of computers on a bus that then is driven to a place where the respondents are asked to come to answer the questions. In the bus, many interviews can be done simultaneously under the supervision of one researcher. This was the system used by Gavrilov in the farmlands of the Soviet Union. Another possibility, which will be discussed below, is to organize completely automatic interview procedures.

In order to make the CAPI procedure truly efficient, one must provide the interviewer with a modem by which the interviews can be sent from the central computer to the computer of the interviewer and the data returned to the central computer. This can be done during the night or in the morning when no other activities take place. As a result, mailing costs are considerably reduced, the speed of research is increased, and one has better control of the sample.

The latest developments in the field of CADAC have taken place in panel-survey research (repeated observations of the same cases of the population). Panel-survey research normally is done by a mixture of face-to-face interviewing, telephone interviewing, and write-in procedures (diaries). The development of computer-assisted interviewing also has created new possibilities for panel research. One possibility is the collection of the data by CATI or CAPI, or by a mixture of both procedures. In these procedures, interviewers play an important role. The role of the interviewer is considerably reduced if self-administered interviews are used.

There also have been developments toward completely automatic panel-survey research. This has been done in several ways. Clemens (1984) has reported experiments with the Prestel videotex system in the United Kingdom, where respondents answer on-line, in self-administered mode, questions that appear on the screen of the terminals in their homes. Kiesler and Sproull (1986) have reported on an experimental research project where an ad-hoc sample of computer users, connected to a computer network, answered questions on the computer available to them. De Pijper and Saris (1986a) have developed one of the more successful systems in this class, the "tele-interviewing." In this system, a random sample of the population is provided with a home computer and modem. With this hardware and a normal telephone, it is possible to send an interview from a central computer to the home computer or PC of the respondent. The respondent answers the questions on the computer, and afterward the answers automatically are returned. The advantage of this procedure is that interviewers are required only to ask the subjects for their cooperation and to explain the procedure. After that first contact, the respondents can answer all questions on the home computer, and the interviewer is no longer needed. This system has been tested successfully by the Sociometric Research Foundation (de Pijper and Saris, 1986b) and has been applied in commercial research by the Dutch Gallup Organization since 1986 with a sample of 1,000 households (van Doorn, 1987-1988). At the moment, a similar panel with a sample of 2,400 households has been set up by the University of Amsterdam.

TABLE 2.1
A Classification of CADAC Procedures

Name	Description	Role of Interviewer	Observation
CATI	computer- assisted telephone interviewing	interviewer - administered	ad hoc and repeated
CAPI	computer-assisted personal interviewing	interviewer or self-administered	ad hoc and repeated
TI	tele-interview using PCs and modems	self-administered	repeated
PDE	prepared data entry	self-administered	repeated
TDE	touchtone data entry	self administered	repeated
VRE	voice recognition entry	self-administered	repeated

An alternative procedure for tele-interviewing has been developed in the United States and is known as *prepared data entry* (PDE). Since 1988, the Energy Information Administration in the United States has asked firms to provide information via a PC interview. In some cases, the information is sent to the central computer by mail. In other cases, the transport of data is done electronically.

There are two further procedures that were developed for business research and are completely automatized. These two systems are called *touchtone data entry* (TDE) and *voice recognition entry* (VRE). In both systems, the computer reads questions from a record and the respondent has to answer by use of the telephone. The first system requires a touchtone telephone that allows numeric answers to be typed. The second system allows the respondents to speak into the telephone directly, and the computer at the other side tries to recognize the numeric answers (Clayton and Harrel, 1989; Winter and Clayton, 1990). Although both systems are operational and have great potential, especially the VRE, it is still too early to predict their future. At the moment, they can only be used for very short interviews with respondents who are familiar with the system.

In Table 2.1, the information about the most important systems has been summarized. This table also indicates whether or not interviewers are needed for data collection, and whether the system can be used for ad hoc research or only for repeated observations of the same cases. These two features of the systems are mentioned because they are much more important in describing different CADAC systems than the technology that has been used in the different systems.

As can be seen from this overview, computer-assisted panel research (CAPAR) can be interviewer-administered in the case of CATI or CAPI, and also self-administered in the form of CAPI, tele-interview (TI), PDE, TDE and VRE. Cross-sectional surveys can be done by CATI and CAPI, but systems that can collect data from a fixed panel repeatedly also can be used for description of a situation at a specific moment. So the technology does not differentiate between the different possible applications.

On the other hand, we will argue that interviewer-administered and self-administered interviews require very different approaches by the interview designer in order to get good quality interviews. We also will show that repeated observations allow much more quality control in the interviews, but require much more effort. Given that we want to discuss procedures to improve data quality, we will distinguish between procedures for cross-sectional surveys and panel surveys, and between procedures for interviewer-administered and self-administered CADAC, and will not concentrate so much on the technology required. (A few words on this point will be said in the last chapter.)

Interviewer-Administered Survey Research

As we already have mentioned, we will discuss two different procedures in this monograph: CATI, which is by necessity an interviewer-administered procedure; and CAPI, as far as the interviewer plays an active role. Because both procedures are CADAC procedures, they have all the advantages and disadvantages of these procedures mentioned in the first chapter. However, these two procedures have several characteristics in common due to their use of interviewer-administered questionnaires. We concentrate on these characteristics in the next section.

Complex Questions and Answer Categories. One of these characteristics, a very general one not necessarily connected with the computer aspect of the procedure, concerns the fact that it is very difficult for respondents to memorize a large series of possible alternative answers or a very long instruction read to them by the interviewer. This problem is mentioned here

32

because it is one of the differences between this procedure and those discussed later.

Two examples can illustrate this point. The first example is a common question about the political agenda:

What is, according to you, the most important political issue at the moment?

1. Unemployment
2. Pollution
3. Danger of a nuclear war
4. Poverty in the Third World
5. AIDS
6. Crime in the cities
7. Homeless people
8. Drugs
9. Danger of catastrophes
10. Terrorism

If one tries such a question in an interviewer-administered questionnaire, two reactions occur very frequently. First, many respondents ask the interviewer to repeat the question again. Second, the respondent often says "the first" or "the last" issue. The first reaction clearly indicates that the respondent could not remember all the options that had just been read to him or her. The second reaction leaves this interpretation open. It is possible that this is a serious answer, but it is more likely that the respondent has given this answer in order to avoid repetition of the question, which would take more time, and which could also give the bad impression that he or she is not able to remember all the options.

One might think that in such a situation it is probably better not to read the possible answers to the respondent, making it an open question instead. However, research by Schuman and Presser (1981) and Billiet et al. (1984) has indicated that quite different results are obtained if such an open question is used. A better alternative, if one is interested in the differences in the relative importance of the different issues and not in the individual responses, is to randomize the order in which the options are read to the respondent.

This option exists in CADAC procedures, but not in normal interviews. In this way, at least on an aggregate level, reasonable results are obtained.

A similar problem exists if the instruction is very long. The next example illustrates this point:

> Political parties differ in their political orientation. Some are more right-wing oriented and others more left-wing. We would like to ask you to evaluate the political orientation of the different parties. An extreme left-wing position is indicated by zero and an extreme right-wing position by 100. We ask you to express your opinion about the parties' positions with a number. So, how would you then evaluate the position of the . . . ?

Again, a common reaction to this question is that the respondents ask: "Can you say it again?" or "what did you say: right-wing is zero and left-wing is 100?" Or they start to answer the question and reverse the direction of the scale. In this case, there is little one can do except repeat the reference points once more just before they start to answer.

These problems are typical of all interviews where the interviewer reads the questions to the respondent. Such questions must not be long or complex; otherwise the respondents cannot remember the necessary information. In self-administered questionnaires this problem is less severe, because the respondents are able to look back in the text. An alternative is the use of show cards during the interview, but this is possible only in CAPI applications; also, it would mean that the interviewer would have to carry a computer *and* a pack of cards, which would increase considerably the weight he or she must carry. Thornberry et al. (1990) found that this is still a problem. The introduction of the notebook computers in the near future will considerably reduce this problem. In the long run, it is not impossible that this situation also will improve for CATI systems, if drastically different telephone networks (ISDN) are introduced that will allow pictures to be transmitted from the interviewer to the respondent at a speed of 64 KB per second. There is even a possibility of a system (broadband-ISDN) that is 10,000 times faster (Gonzalez, 1990). These developments suggest that in the future, the problem of the visual aids will be solved for CAPI as well as CATI; however, at the moment one has to recognize that the problem of complex questions and instructions exists in interviewer-administered interviews.

Due to the recent changes in Eastern Europe, a suggestion has been made that the NATO and Warsaw Pact countries should draw up new treaties governing the first use of nuclear weapons.

What do you think of a proposal whereby both parties would agree never to use nuclear weapons as a first-strike weapon ?

(A first strike is intended to destroy the other country, so that it cannot attack so easily any more. For an explaination of NATO and WARSAW PACT press F3.)

  1 agree
  2 disagree
  9 don't know

Figure 2.1. Example 5

Help by the Interviewer. A positive feature of the procedures where the interviewer plays an important role is that the interviewer can help the respondent to understand the questions correctly and give the appropriate answer. In CADAC procedures these possibilities also exist, but it is more difficult for the interviewer to be of much help: The questionnaires can be so structured with respect to branching and skipping in the questionnaire that each interview looks very different to the interviewer. In this case, the interviewer is hardly more likely than the respondent to be able to understand the questions, unless intensive training has been given to the interviewers.

Nevertheless, no matter how much training is given to the interviewers, it is always very wise in designing CADAC interviewer-administered questionnaires to provide the interviewer with as much information as possible to give him or her a better understanding of the meaning of the question. This extra information can be given on the screen where the question is presented, or on a separate help screen that is only called up if necessary. We will illustrate this point with an example.

There are situations where it makes sense to provide help information on the screen for all interviewers, because it is likely that only a few of them will know that information. An example is the military use of the *first-strike* concept. If an opinion about the first-strike capabilities of NATO (North Atlantic Treaty Organization) is requested, it is probably wise to explain the concept of first strike to all interviewers and respondents.

There are also situations in which the interviewer and the respondent usually will know what is meant by the terms used, but occasionally will need further information. For example, if the questionnaire asks people for their opinions about NATO, many people will know what this organization is, but some people might need help. In a case like this, help should be given on a separate help screen in order to avoid overcrowded screens. Example 5 (Figure 2.1) illustrates this possibility.

This example illustrates how in CADAC procedures extra information can be supplied that interviewers need in order to be helpful to the respondent. The information can be given directly on the screens to all interviewers, or it can be given only to those people who need the information. In the latter case, help screens that only appear on request are used. In order to obtain this extra information, the interviewer must press some key (i.e., the function key F3).

Example 5 (Figure 2.1), however, also illustrates that help could be given directly to the respondent without being presented by the interviewer. Only occasionally will the interviewer play an important role, namely when the questionnaire is not very suitable for the respondent and all kinds of problems arise. However, even in these situations, the interviewer cannot do very much because of the relatively rigid structure of CADAC procedures. We will return to this point later.

Keeping Up the Pace of the Interview. A very important aspect of interviewing, especially of telephone interviewing, is that there should only be a very short time between questions. If the delay is more than a few seconds, respondents can get annoyed and withdraw their cooperation or reduce it to the minimum (House, 1985). This can have very negative effects on the quality of the data. The speed with which the interviewer can move from one screen to the next depends on (a) the quality of the hardware and software, (b) the activities that are organized between two questions, (c) the layout of the screens, (d) the difficulty the interviewer has with corrections, and (e) the flexibility of the questionnaire or program in the event of serious problems arising. A similar list of points has been given by House (1985) for CATI interviewing, but many of the arguments given for CATI can be generalized to other applications as well. Let us look at these different points more closely.

First of all, *the replacement of one screen by another* is dependent on the quality of the hardware and the software. If the interviews are done on a terminal connected to a central computer, the response time can be rather slow when other users are making use of the same computer. But even if a personal computer is used, the response time can be slow due to the way the software is operating. Delays are mostly due to reading from and writing to the diskettes, or to very complex codings or calculations. If a program is reading or writing all the time, the process is slowed down. Such delays can be considerably reduced by writing to and reading from a RAM (random-access memory) disk instead of a diskette or hard disk. On the other hand, the tasks need to be very complex indeed to slow down a computer due to coding and calculations.

Also, the *design of the questionnaire* can affect the speed of the program. The designer of a questionnaire can increase the pace of the interview considerably by avoiding situations where the computer has to do many different tasks at the same moment between two questions (i.e., coding a complex response, writing the answers to a disk, reading a new part of the interview, making some calculations, and evaluating a complex branching statement). All of these tasks can be designed to happen between two questions, but with a little bit of effort, it often is possible to spread them over several questions, so although some moves may take a little longer, a very long delay is avoided.

A second way in which the questionnaire designer can influence the pace of the interview is by designing *screen layout* procedures that are immediately clear to the interviewer. If the screen is not immediately clear to the interviewer, she or he will need some time to study it before the question can be formulated. House (1985) suggests some important rules to follow:

1. Standard procedures should be used to indicate questions and instructions. For example, questions can be given in normal letters and instructions in inverse video (reverse screen). Words that should be stressed could be underlined or bold; extra information can be given in a different color. Of course, these suggestions are arbitrary; more important is that the interviews should always look the same to the interviewer so that quick orientation is possible.

2. The different parts of the screen should always be used in the same way (e.g., first some short instructions to the interviewer, then, below that, the questions and the response categories, and to the right of the categories extra information if available).

3. The screen should not be too full of text. It is my experience that lines with important information should be separated by blank lines to make them immediately recognizable to the interviewer. If there are many answer categories that need not be read by the interviewer, they can be closer together.

The time between questions certainly will be too long if the answers of the respondents do not fit in the specified categories and there are no facilities for the interviewer to solve these problems. It goes without saying that CADAC questionnaires should be tested thoroughly. But even if this is done, it is unavoidable that once in a while a respondent will give answers that do not fit into the system of the questionnaire. This is one of the major problems with CADAC procedures. The one thing that can be said about it is that one should do the necessary tests (We will come back to this later) and that one should allow for a way out if "impossible" events occur. One way is always to allow an "other" category, with some suggestion of what this other possibility may be. This option requires choices with respect to branching and skipping, which might be complicated. Another possibility is to allow the interviewer to comment at any time (or at frequent intervals) on the responses and possible errors that may have occurred. The disadvantage of this option is that one still has to edit the data after the data collection is done.

Another aspect of the design that can speed up the interview concerns the *procedures to correct inconsistencies*. If these procedures are too complex, the time between the question that led to the contradictory answer and the next question becomes too long. Because this concerns the more general issue of how the interviewer must deal with inconsistencies, this point is discussed further in the next section.

Clearing Up Inconsistencies. As the final point in this section, the general problem of clearing up inconsistencies is discussed. In Chapter 1, we mentioned that this facility of CADAC procedures is one of its major attractions. Nevertheless, these procedures are not without dangers. One has already been mentioned: If the procedure for correcting inconsistencies is not clear to the interviewer, it might take too much time before the next question can be asked.

There are different procedures in use to make these corrections. The start, however, is always the same: The program compares the answers to different questions and detects inconsistencies that cannot be tolerated or finds combinations of answers that are extremely unlikely. But what the program does not and cannot tell is which of the answers is incorrect.

One way to proceed in such a situation is to provide the interviewer with all the available information, point out that there is an inconsistency, and ask him or her to sort it out. If only two questions are involved, this is not very difficult. For example, the program can say:

Question	Answer
Age father	35
Age son (John)	36
Not possible!	

In this case, when the names of the questions are available, it should be clear to the interviewer what must be done.

1. Mention that there is something wrong.
2. Ask for clarification.
3. Go back to the question that has been wrongly answered and correct the answer there.
4. If other questions depend on this answer, these questions also should be asked so that complete and correct data are obtained.
5. Finally, the program should return to the point where the inconsistency was found.

What is not specified in this procedure is how the interviewer should approach this task. Should she or he say:

"You made an error because . . ."
"I am sorry, but there is a difficulty . . ."
"I am sorry, but the computer detected that . . . ," or
"I may have recorded something incorrectly here . . ."

Although the first formulation is correct, one cannot use it too frequently if one wants the respondent to remain motivated.

An additional complication is that it may be not only the age information that is wrong, but also the information about the relationship with the respondent. The name of this question is not on the screen, and the interviewer will have to look for it in order to make the necessary corrections. This can be a complicated matter that takes some time if the question is far away in the questionnaire and there is no easy way to find its name. This is a typical situation in which the time between two questions can become too long, as previously mentioned.

Of course, it would have been better if the designer of the questionnaire had foreseen this possibility and given the name of this question on the screen. In this case, all necessary corrections could be made. If this procedure is used, the sequence of questions and the formulation of them is no longer under the control of the researcher. The interviewers have to decide for themselves which question to correct. Previous research has indicated that they do not necessarily correct the proper questions. Some interviewers chose to correct the question that is simplest to correct, which is often the last one. However, that is not necessarily the appropriate question to correct (van Bastelaer, Kersssemakers, and Sikkel, 1988).

An alternative approach that allows the researcher to maintain complete control is to specify extra questions to deal with all possible inconsistencies. In this case, the interviewer does not have to make decisions about which direction to take. The interview always goes forward, never backward. Of course, the specification of the extra questions is not an easy task, but if one can specify a consistency check one also can specify extra questions. For the problem mentioned above, the designer could present a question next to the given information:

I am sorry, but the computer has detected that in one question you mentioned that your age is 35 and in another that the age of your son John is 36.
Of course, this is very unlikely.
Is your age wrong, is the age of your son wrong, are both wrong, or is there another error (more than one answer is possible)?

1. My age
2. Age of my son John
3. John is not my son
4. Other problem

If one (or both) of the given ages is wrong extra questions about it will follow, and then the normal questioning continues. If John is not his son, a question follows about their relationship.

It will be clear that both procedures have their advantages. The first procedure gives some freedom, but this can be dangerous in the sense that wrong questions are asked or wrong corrections are made for simplicity, or the interview cannot be continued because the name of the question that should be corrected is missing.

The second procedure is more controlled, but also is more rigid. The designer must analyze the problems well in advance. On the other hand, if the designer is not doing this, the first procedure also runs into problems because question names that are needed to jump to the question with the wrong answer are missing.

Monitoring the Behavior of Interviewers. It is inherent in the role of the interviewer in these procedures that the interviewers can do things that the researcher does not wish them to do. At worst, they talk to the wrong person, or falsify interviews or parts of interviews. It is not known how frequently this occurs (Groves and Nicholls, 1986), but all research institutes at some time are confronted with such occurrences.

Less extreme, but also very unpleasant, is the fact that the interviewers have a tendency to change the wording of the questions, partly in anticipation of the answers expected of the respondents (Brenner, 1982; Dijkstra, 1983). In CAPI applications, not much can be done to stop these activities, because it is not easy to control the interviewers except by calling the respondents to verify information. However, although doing so allows the researcher to check whether the interview was or was not completely falsified, it cannot change the way the interview was performed. In the next section, we will discuss various radical solutions to this problem in CAPI applications. In CATI, it is possible to check up on the interviewers. Technically, it is possible not only to monitor their behavior on the phone, but also to copy the text of their screen to the screen of a control computer. In this way, the research management has complete audio- and video-monitoring possibilities. Only samples of the whole process can be monitored, but given that the interviewers are aware of the possibility that their behavior may be observed, they will take more care and not engage in the devastating activities mentioned above, and may even reduce the amount of reformulation of questions. These monitoring facilities are certainly of great value in the CATI applications, even though the monitoring can lead to some stress on the part of the interviewers.

It will have become clear from the discussion in this section that the interviewer-administered CADAC procedures CATI and CAPI have many possibilities, but that good results are not obtained without costs. One must make a considerable investment of time in good questionnaire design. This is especially true for consistency checks and on-line editing. If one wants to use these facilities, a lot of effort and time is required. Whether this is worthwhile for ad-hoc survey research remains to be seen.

Self-Administered Survey Research

The most important difference between the self-administered procedures and the interviewer-administered procedures is the role of the interviewer. In the self-administered surveys, there is no interviewer reading the questions and typing in the answers. If there is an interviewer present during the interview, his or her role is only to clarify general points.

The major advantage of this approach, of course, is that there is no interviewer to change the questions. As a result, all respondents are presented with the same questions and the same answer categories. This does not mean that all respondents will read the text equally carefully, but (at least from a researcher's point of view) the presentation is optimal, because one can completely determine which information, questions, instructions, and answer categories are presented to the respondents.

Although this is a very attractive situation, it also requires a lot of effort on the part of the questionnaire designer, who cannot rely on an interviewer for clarification. The whole process needs to be spelled out well in advance. Also, given that some people have only limited reading and writing abilities, and even less computer experience, the procedures must be very simple so that anybody can do the interviews. The requirements for such an approach will be the topic of this section. We also will discuss other aspects specific to the self-administered questionnaire that can help the respondents in their work. The tools that can be provided may be so efficient that they more than compensate for the absence of an interviewer: visual aids, calendars, summary and correction (SC) screens, more complex category scales, the use of psychophysical scales, and complex instructions.

User-Friendliness. Self-administered questionnaires require much more user-friendliness from the interview program and questionnaire than interviewer-administered procedures. Although programs that can be done by the respondents themselves also can be done by interviewers, the opposite is not always true. In particular, the instructions and consistency checks are quite different in self-administered questionnaires.

Let us first discuss the instructions. Clearly, one cannot give instructions like "Do not read the categories" if one would like to ask an "unaided recall" question. Such a question should be presented as an open question in these procedures. But if it were a real open question, routing would be impossible. Therefore, the answers have to be coded immediately, using a dictionary specified by the researcher. After coding in several categories, further branching is possible.

A typical example of such a question would be a question asking respondents to mention names of cigarette brands to see which are the best known. Next, the people are asked if they know those brand names that they did not mention. An illustration of such a questionnaire is presented in Example 6 (Figure 2.2).

This example is a little bit complicated using the language of the INTERV program, because the program does not provide a standard procedure for this type of questionnaire. But the result is the same as that achieved automatically in other programs.

# of questions=1
Type=code Var=V1
    Please give the name of the first
    brand of cigarettes that comes
    to your mind ?
    Codes: 1 "pall mal" "pal mal" "pal mall" "pall mall"
            2 "marboro" "mar_" "marlboro"
            3 "luck_" "_strike" "lucky strike"
            4 "camal" "cammel" "camell" "camel"
Calculation
V20=1
Repeat 5
Calculation
V20=V20+1
# of questions 1
Type=code var=V[V20]
    If you know more names
    type another name below.
    Otherwise type: NO
    Codes: 1 "pall mal" "pal mal" "pal mall" "pall mall"
            2 "marboro" "mar_" "marlboro"
            3 "lucky _" "_strike" "lucky strike"
            4 "camal" "cammel" "camell" "camel"
            5 "NO"
Until (V[V20]=5)
Calculation
V11=0   V12=0   V13=0   V14=0
[v1=1 or v2=1 or v3=1 or v4=1 or v5=1] V11=1
[v1=2 or v2=2 or v3=2 or v4=2 or v5=2] V12=1
[v1=3 or v2=3 or v3=3 or v4=3 or v5=3] V13=1
[v1=4 or v2=4 or v3=4 or v4=4 or v5=4] V14=1
# of questions=1
Type=multi range=[1 4] var=aided
    Which of the following brands have you also heard of ?
Condition V11=0
    {1. Pal Mall}
Condition V12=0
    {2. Marlboro}
Condition V13=0
    {3. Lucky Strike}
Condition V14=0
    {4. Camel}
    You can mention more than one brand.
    Type a number after each number
    and press F5 at the end.
END

Figure 2.2. Example 6

> Please give the name of the first
> brand of cigarettes that comes
> to your mind ?

Figure 2.3. Screen 1 of Example 6

The first question presented on the screen will be the question in Screen 1 of Example 6 (Figure 2.3). Notice that the dictionary from the question text is not presented. After the first question, a second question is repeated maximally five times. This second question asks for other brand names. This is also an unaided recall question, because the names of the brands are not mentioned on the screen, only in the dictionary. This "repeat until" procedure stops before the fifth round if the respondent answers "no" on the second question, meaning that she or he knows no other names.

Now imagine that the respondent mentioned the names *Pall Mall* and *Lucky Strike*. Then the next step is that in a calculation block the variables V11 and V13 obtain the value 1, and the variables V12 and V14 will have the value 0.

After that calculation, the last question is presented. Only the names of those brands that were not mentioned by the respondent are presented, as shown in Screen 2 of Example 6 (Figure 2.4). The last question is a multiple-response question by means of which the respondents can indicate which names of brands they can remember in aided recall.

> Which of the following brands
> have you also heard of ?
>
> 2. Marlboro
> 4. Camel

Figure 2.4. Screen 2 of Example 6

This is a typical example of how instructions and procedures are changed to make up for the fact that there is no interviewer present. On the one hand, the procedure becomes more difficult for the researcher to write, whereas on the other hand, the procedure for the respondents becomes simpler.

Example 6 (Figure 2.2) also illustrates the point that this procedure can be used in self-administered and interviewer-administered interviews, but the interviewer-administered version with the instruction to the interviewer not to read the specified categories cannot be used in the self-administered procedures.

The same complications occur with respect to the consistency checks. The previous section showed two procedures to deal with inconsistencies. One was interviewer-dependent, as the interviewer just got a message that inconsistencies had occurred, and the names of the questions involved were presented. It was then up to the interviewer to decide how to solve these inconsistencies. This procedure cannot be used in self-administered interviews.

The second procedure took into account all possible errors and proposed several specific questions to solve the inconsistency. It is this procedure that should be used for self-administered interviews. Again, procedures for self-administered interviewing, being more explicit, can be used in interviewer-administered procedures, but not vice versa.

Use of Visual Aids. One of the procedures frequently used to improve data quality is the use of visual aids. As seen above, the use of these tools is not possible in the CATI application and is difficult in CAPI applications that are interviewer-administered, but in self-administered procedures they can be used.

An example would be the use of pictures to help respondents remember whether they have seen or read a newspaper or magazine, whether they know a certain person, and so forth. In media research, such aids play an important role. For example, if one would like to know if people have seen the latest edition of a magazine, it is often very difficult without visual aids for them to remember whether they have seen it. They may not know whether the last issue they have seen was from this week or last week. If, however, the front page of the magazine is shown and they are asked to say whether they have seen it, it is easier for the respondent to answer the question correctly.

Technically, the application of these procedures in self-administered questionnaires is not difficult. The pictures can be scanned and stored on the interview diskette. In the question text, an instruction can be given that the picture can be obtained by pressing a function key (Sociometric Research Foundation, 1988). When the key is pressed, the picture appears on the screen, and when the respondent wants to return to the questionnaire, the same function key is pressed again. If the picture does not cover the whole screen, it also can be integrated into the questionnaire text, with the question text around the picture. With modern text processors, these procedures are not too difficult, but they do take time.

The fact that the pictures require a lot of space in memory and on the diskettes can cause problems. A full-sized picture requires 64 KB. One solution is to combine several pictures on one screen, which would still require 64 KB but now for, say, four pictures instead of one. Another possibility would be to use pictures that are smaller than a full screen. A third possibility is to use the larger storage capacities of hard disks, although this would be much more expensive.

Use of a Calendar. Another application of visual aids is the use of calendars in interviews. In the literature, the problems of memory effect, complete loss of memory, and telescoping have been mentioned frequently (e.g., Sikkel, 1985; Sudman and Bradburn, 1974). The solution to this problem suggested in the literature is to offer reference points in time by providing a calendar. In interviewer-administered interviews this is too difficult, but in self-administered interviews it is no problem; the procedure can be organized in the same way as for the pictures in the previous example. If the respondent presses a function key, the calendar is shown, and if he or she presses it again, the calendar disappears, and the program returns to the appropriate question in the questionnaire (Kersten, 1988). Various well-known events can be noted in the calendar, such as national holidays (e.g., Memorial Day) and religious feasts (e.g., Christmas); the birthdays of the respondent and other members of the household also can be included if this information is available. With these dates fixed in the calendar, it has been suggested that other activities, such as visits to the doctor, purchases, or other behavior, can be located more precisely in time (Loftus and Marburger, 1983).

Summary and Correction Screens. A similar tool to improve the quality of the data in self-administered interviews is the *summary and correction screen,* or SC screen. In Chapter 1, we mentioned that CADAC has the disadvantage that respondents and interviewers face the problem that the answers are typed on the keyboard but the questions are presented on the screen, which might lead to errors in the responses. Also, for other reasons, errors can occur in the data. These errors might remain undetected by range checks and consistency checks because they represent plausible answers, but these answers may be incorrect nevertheless. If branching and skipping depend on these answers, this might lead to problems later in the interview. Therefore, SC screens have been developed (Kersten, Verweij, Hartman, and Gallhofer, 1990). These screens summarize important responses and allow the respondent to make corrections. These procedures are especially useful before important branching decisions are made.

A typical example of such a situation is information on the household. If this information about the members of the household and their ages is to be used later on in the interview, (e.g., to select the persons who should be asked for further information about their work hours in the past week), it is very important that the basic household information is correct, or problems will arise.

These problems can be twofold. The less difficult problem is that for one person the information is not requested, when it should have been. The second, more serious problem that can arise is that information is requested about a certain person when this person is, for example, too young to work. In such a situation, the respondent will have problems if no easy way out is provided. However, if the information was requested far back in the questionnaire, returning to the question is very difficult. In this case, the respondent has serious problems.

In order to avoid such problems, the vital information used for later branching should be summarized in an SC screen, and the respondent should be asked to check the information once more very carefully. It would take too much space to show the whole procedure here, but a typical SC screen for a household with four people (two parents and two children) is presented in Figure 2.5.

For the lines that are incorrect, questions about the name and age follow again. Then the SC screen is given again, and this procedure is repeated until the respondent is satisfied with the result. This procedure does not give a complete guarantee of the correctness of the data, but it certainly ensures the quality of the data better than procedures that do not use SC screens.

Psychophysical Scaling. The previous section showed that interviewer-administered interviews cannot make use of scales with many categories unless show cards are used, because respondents cannot remember all the categories that have been read to them. In self-administered procedures this is not a problem, because the respondents can always look back. They have the time and all the information in front of them. This means that this limitation does not apply to the procedures discussed here. However, not only can questions with many categories be used, but also there are possibilities that are completely out of the question in interviewer-administered

Person	Age
(1) John	40
(2) Mary	39
(3) Harry	17
(4) Lucy	12

Please check carefully whether the names
and ages of the people in the table are correct
because other questions depend on this
information being correct.

If all information is correct, type 0
and press F5

If lines are incorrect type their numbers
with a return in between
and press F5.

Figure 2.5. Typical SC Screen for Household of Four People

interviews. These possibilities include the use of all kinds of scales that make use of some kind of response manipulations by the respondent. Some examples of such scales are analogue-rating scales, line-production scales, sound-production scales, and other psychophysical scales (Lodge, 1981; Saris, 1982; Stevens, 1975; Wegener, 1982).

These scales have an advantage over the commonly used categorical scales in that they allow the respondents to express their opinions on continuous scales. This allows more precision in expressing their opinions (Lodge, 1981). This is an important point, because van Doorn, Saris, and Lodge, (1983) and Költringer (1991) have shown that the categorization of theoretically continuous variables can lead to considerable bias in the estimates of the strength of relations between variables.

The attraction of the CADAC procedures for these scaling purposes is that one can ask the respondents to express their opinions through the length of lines that are automatically measured by the computer. This way, one does not have to rely on manual measurement, as was done in early experiments with psychophysical scales (see Lodge, Cross, Tursky, and Tanenhaus, 1975).

Furthermore, the availability of different modalities for the expression of opinions makes it easier to ask respondents to express their opinion twice, in different modalities. These repeated observations make it easier to correct for unavoidable measurement errors without reducing the validity of the measures. For detailed discussion of these points, see the psychometric literature (e.g., Lord and Novick, 1968) and sociometric literature (e.g., Andrews, 1984; Saris, 1982; Saris and Andrews, in press).

These procedures are not without problems, however, due to the variability in the way people answer questions. Each respondent can use his or her own scale to express his or her opinions, but due to this variation in the response scales (or as Saris, 1988, has called it, the variation in the response functions), the scores obtained for the different respondents are not comparable. In order to remedy this point, more complex instructions to the respondents are necessary. A previous section showed that complex instructions can lead to problems in interviewer-administered interviews, but not as much as in self-administered interviews. The following section will deal with complex instructions, and so also will illustrate the psychophysical scales.

Complex Instructions. Psychophysical scaling (and other questions) requires a complex instruction, which could lead to problems in interviewer-administered interviews, but not in self-administered questionnaires. The reason is the same as before: respondents can look back and find very quickly what they have forgotten. We will illustrate this point with an example of psychophysical scaling, taking into account the problem of variation in response functions across respondents. Bon (1988) has shown that it is impossible to correct for the variation in the response functions. Therefore, if one wishes to use individual data or the study of relationships between variables, the only possible solution is to prevent the variation in response functions as far as possible. Experiments by Saris, van de Putte, Maas, and Seip (1988), Batista and Saris (1988), and Saris and de Rooy (1988) have made it clear that providing respondents with not one reference point, as is commonly done, but two reference points with a fixed meaning will improve the data considerably. In other words, these authors suggest that instructions like the one below should be used:

We are now going to ask your opinion about a number of issues. If you are in complete agreement with the expressed opinion, draw a line of the following length:

_____

If you completely disagree with an opinion, draw a line like this:

___

The more you agree, the longer the line you should draw.

Although clearly such a scale is not possible in an interviewer-administered interview because of the use of line production, the instruction is still too complicated even if magnitude estimation is used instead of line production.

The above scale has been used for many years with very good results, frequently leading to reliabilities of 0.90 to 0.95, which is very high compared with other scales (Saris, 1989). One of the reasons for these good results is the extra precision of the 38-point scale. Another reason is that the scale is fixed by two reference points.

This overview has shown that the self-administered questionnaire has quite a number of advantages over the interviewer-administered interview. In the previous section, we described some procedures that can help keep the quality high. In this section, we pointed to several procedures that can improve the quality. But, again, these advantages are not obtained for free. They require extra effort from the designer of the questionnaire. The formulation demands more effort and time. And it is not only the writing of the questionnaire that requires extra time, but the testing of the questionnaire as well.

One of the reasons why testing is necessary is that help screens are essential components of these questionnaires, and the best place for these help screens can only be found through tests. How the tests are carried out will be discussed later.

Computer-Assisted Panel Research

As mentioned previously, computer-assisted panel research can be done by CATI, CAPI, computer-assisted mail interviewing (CAMI), tele-interviewing, or videotext systems. The rest of this chapter will concentrate on the continuous character of panel research and on the possibilities it offers to improve the quality of the data collection if any type of CADAC is used. In this section, we will return to several topics already mentioned, but with the difference that we now will be making use of a continuous stream of information about the same persons. This means that not only information about background variables, but also information about several important variables at different points in time will be available. A typical example of research where such a situation occurs is the ongoing family expenditure studies that are carried out in many countries and that normally are done by a combination of personal interviews and self-administered diaries.

In order to refine these procedures, some new facilities have been developed, which can be classified into two groups: procedures with the aim of directly reducing the number of errors, and procedures designed to reduce the amount of effort on the part of the respondent. The second type of procedure also may lead to a reduction in the number of errors, but only indirectly. We will discuss both types of procedures.

New Procedures for Data Validation. The most common procedures for data validation or editing are range checks and consistency checks across time. In paper-and-pencil interviews, these checks are performed after the data have been collected. At that moment, when the respondent is no longer available, errors are difficult to correct, but at least one can clean the data and eventually assign some values for erroneous answers on the basis of some more or less plausible assumptions.

A fundamental difference with computer-assisted interviewing is that the checks are all performed during the interview while the respondent is still present. This means that the respondent can immediately correct any errors. If all the possible and necessary checks are done during the interview, the validation phase after the data collection can be eliminated, or at least considerably reduced.

All the procedures discussed so far use data from one interview. In panel research, one gets an extra source of information to check the quality of the data, namely, the information from the previous interview(s). Validation procedures that use this information are dynamic range and consistency checks, dynamic SC screens, and dynamic calendars. We will discuss these different procedures in sequence.

Dynamic Range and Consistency Checks. Range checks are checks that are based on prior knowledge of the possible answers. For example, if the question is about the prices of different products, it is easy to type in "200" instead of "20"; such errors can lead to values that are too high by a factor of 10 or more. Most interview programs have the facility to specify range checks on the answers. For example, the program INTERV can specify a lower and an upper bound for continuous responses. If the program detects an answer outside the acceptable range, it automatically mentions at the bottom of the screen that the answer should be within the specified range and the response is ignored, which means that the respondent has to answer again.

These range checks are "hard checks" in the sense that one cannot continue with the next question until an answer is given that falls within the acceptable range. It will be clear that one should be very careful with these hard checks in order to avoid problems. This means that they are normally only used for checks on obvious typing errors, where it is certain that the answer is wrong.

A second type of check that can be performed and that is also available in most interview programs is to specify the conditions under which a question is presented. This procedure can be used for consistency checks, because these checks are used as conditions for questions that ask for clarification. We have discussed these possibilities before, but will give another example. If we are interested in people's income, we might ask those who work the following question:

Type=price range=[1   200,000] var=income
How much did you earn last month?

In the Netherlands, we would expect an answer between 1,000 and, say, 10,000 gulden (one U.S. dollar equals approximately two guldens). All answers outside this range are very unlikely, but not impossible. This means that we cannot do a range check using these values. A range check can only be done with the values 1 and perhaps 200,000.

But in order to have a more sensitive check, we can use a "soft check," which consists of a conditional question only asked if the answer to the first question is below 1,000 gulden and above, for example, 5,000 gulden. The extra question would be

Type=price var=check
Condition (1000>income or income>5000)
You gave a very unlikely income of "income "
If you made a mistake, press F1 and answer the question again. If the answer is correct go on to the next question by pressing ENTER.

This example shows that this is not a hard check. The answer may be correct even though it is very deviant, and in that case the respondent can go on; but in 99% of cases the answers will be wrong, and the respondent is given a chance to correct the error.

The latter checking procedure is already much more flexible than the range check, but it is still very rough and can be annoying for people with a very deviant income, because in a panel study they will get the correction question each time their income is requested. This is neither necessary nor desirable, and should be avoided so as not to annoy the respondent.

Therefore, a dynamic range check should be used that adapts to the information given through time, on the basis that the information about a person at time t is often the same as at time $t - 1$. Thus, if the information about income at t can be saved and used the next time, this would be the most efficient check on the answers in an interview. The above specified procedure could then be adjusted as follows:

Type=price var=check
Condition {(.9*income(t-1)>income) or (1.1*income(t-1)<income)}
You gave a very unlikely income of "income
whereas, last time your income was "income(t-1)
If you made a mistake, press F1 and answer the question again. If the answer is correct, go on to the next question.

Now, the check question is asked whenever the income has been changed by more than 10%, but not if the income is deviant but stable. We consider this to be the most efficient way of making checks, for the following reasons: (a) The range specified can be as narrow as one wishes, (b) it uses as much information as possible from the respondent, (c) people with a constant but deviant position are not bothered all the time by check questions, and (d) the check adjusts itself automatically to a changing situation. If someone's income changes, the check will be adjusted the next time, too.

Here we have given the example of an income question, but the same procedures can be used for many more variables, such as expenditure components (Hartman and Saris, 1991).

Dynamic SC screens. A second general procedure that has been developed to provide possibilities for error correction is the use of SC screens. In panel research, these procedures differ from the SC screens in cross-sectional research in that information from a previous wave can be used.

Let us continue with the example of the income question to illustrate this possibility. If we ask a household for the first time about their incomes, and three out of five people in the household have an income, a typical answer

Person	Income Last Month
(1) John	2,000
(2) Mary	9,000
(3) Harry	1,200
(4) Anna	0
(5) Elizabeth	0

If there is anything wrong in this summary, type the numbers of the lines that are incorrect with a return in between: press F5 if your answer is finished.

If nothing is wrong, press 0 and F5 to continue.

Figure 2.6. An Example of a SC Screen

could be like the one shown in Figure 2.6. This example illustrates a situation where it is possible that all information is correct, but where it is also possible that Mary's income is 10 times too high due to a typing error. The respondent who is filling in the questionnaire will spot this error immediately and correct it, whereas there is no way a program can detect the error if it is the first interview. Furthermore, the next time the question of Mary's income arises, the dynamic range check will assume that her income is 9,000 gulden and will start to complain if the answer given is 900. As this could lead to confusion, the information should be checked before it is used in the next interview. The SC screen provides an easy way to make these corrections.

In panel research, SC screens can be used very efficiently if they are slightly adjusted. Providing the respondents immediately with information about the previous wave and asking them for corrections may prevent errors. The previous example would be adjusted in the manner indicated in Figure 2.7.

The purpose of this procedure is to prevent typing errors as much as possible and to reduce the effort for the respondent. Both purposes are realized by prespecifying, on the basis of the existing information, the most likely answer. If no change has occurred the respondent has only to type a "0" and to press RETURN to answer for all household members the questions about their incomes. If one of the incomes has changed only that income needs to be corrected, and not all incomes must be specified again.

```
According to our information the members
of your household had the following incomes:

Person                  Income in
                        September

(1)  John                   2,000
(2)  Mary                     900
(3)  Harry                  1,200
(4)  Anna                       0
(5)  Elizabeth                  0

If the incomes have changed in October, press the
numbers of the lines that are incorrect with
a return in between; press F5 if your
answer is finished.

If all the incomes remain the same, press 0 and F5 to continue.
```

Figure 2.7. An Example of a Dynamic SC Screen

In this way the respondent's task is made easier, as discussed below, but more important, one can avoid many typing errors without reducing the possibility of specifying changes. The procedure also is designed in such a way that changes through time automatically are taken into account. For this reason, it is called a *dynamic* SC screen.

A Dynamic Calendar. In a previous section, the possibility of preventing errors due to memory failure by using a calendar was mentioned, including public holidays and personal information that could be found in the background variables. However, in panel research, one is getting much more information through time. For example, it is possible to mention in the calendar specific events like visits to the hospital by a family member, a change of job, a special party, or any other event that has been mentioned by the respondents as important. The introduction of these events into the calendar gives the respondents many more reference points to determine when other specific events occurred. The information about these events can be collected during the panel study in other surveys. It is also possible to build up this information from questionnaires on different topics, such as school career, working career, and so forth.

Such procedures might be especially attractive for collecting information about life histories, which is a very popular topic in sociology nowadays.

Life histories are very difficult to specify without memory aids. A calendar full of information about events in the life of the respondent might be a very useful tool for improving the data quality in these studies.

Procedures to Reduce the Work for Respondents. Having discussed several procedures for the detection and correction of errors in the data, we now present some procedures to reduce the workload of the respondents. These procedures do not prevent or correct errors directly, but it can be expected that reducing the workload of the respondents will improve the data they provide and reduce their reluctance to cooperate in unattractive questionnaires. Here, we discuss three different approaches: the use of dynamic SC screens, scheduling, and grouping in SC screens.

The Use of Dynamic SC Screens. In paper-and-pencil questionnaires the possibilities for branching are very limited. Therefore, a large number of questions are printed and asked that do no apply to a specific person. For example, if a person has a pension and is not working anymore, all questions with respect to income from work, holiday money, overtime, and so on, do not apply. Nevertheless, in paper-and-pencil interviews these questions still exist, and it is up to the interviewer to determine which to skip and which to ask. If the conditions for skipping are very simple, an interviewer can do the job, but the interviewer does not have the time or the capability to evaluate complex conditions.

In computer-assisted interviewing, any level of complex branching is possible as long as the researcher understands what she or he is doing. The advantages of automatic branching in the questionnaire are that no errors occur in the branching, thus avoiding partial nonresponse, and that the amount of text the respondent has to read is reduced.

For the pensioner mentioned above, all questions about work as a source of income are automatically skipped, reducing the number of questions considerably. The same kind of approach can be used for information about the household, work, the home, the children's school, and so forth.

However, in panel research one has to take into account that the composition of the household can change, that people may change jobs, move to another house, and so on. This means that it is not enough to request this information once. The information has to be updated in order to prevent errors when it is used for branching in other questionnaires. For this purpose, SC screens are very useful because they allow a very brief summary of the information and allow quick updates. For example, the household information can be summarized in a screen such as the one shown in Figure 2.8.

> According to our records, your situation was as follows in the last interview. Please check if the situation is still the same.
>
> | Person | Work/School | #hours | Where |
> |---|---|---|---|
> | (1) John | work | 38 | university |
> | (2) Anna | work | 22 | school |
> | (3) Harry | work | 38 | Philips |
> | (4) Mary | school | — | secondary |
> | (5) Elizabeth | school | — | primary |
>
> If there is anything wrong in this summary, press the numbers of the lines that are incorrect with a return in between; press F5 if your answer is finished.
>
> If nothing is wrong, press 0 and F5 to continue.

Figure 2.8. An SC Screen of the Household Box Information

In this way, this information does not have to be requested again. The information from the last interview is presented and the respondents can immediately see whether or not there has been any change in their situation since the last interview; if so, they can give their new situation by replying to a few follow-up questions. After this check, which normally takes less than a minute, the updated information can be used for the rest of the interview.

Clearly, this procedure is very efficient, especially in panel research, and will save the respondents a lot of effort, leaving them to concentrate on the new questions and, most likely, to answer them with more precision and care.

Scheduling. Background information can be used not only to reduce the number of questions asked, but also to evaluate the regularity of information that is collected. For example, in the Netherlands, family allowance money comes only once every 3 months, and the telephone bill must be paid only once every 3 months. The same might be true for mortgages, energy bills, and so forth, and often insurance is paid only once a year. Membership fees for different organizations will fall due at different times, but in general there will be a fixed sequence of months in which payment is required. If detailed information is requested once, so that not only the amount is known, but also when the last payment was made and how many months it covered, then an intelligent interview program can calculate the next time that the same payment has to be made. If the amount to be paid is stored, the program can even mention something such as the following:

According to our calculations, last month you had to pay your mortgages, and the amount you had to pay was ___ gulden.
Did you indeed pay this amount last month?
1 = yes.
0 = no.

If the answer is "no," extra questions are asked about the reasons for the change, but normally the amounts and timing will be correct. This way, the amount of effort required of the respondent is much less than when all the different regular expenditures have to be evaluated in the traditional way.

In the months when there is no payment to be made, the work is reduced even further, because in those months the question can be skipped completely, or one can use the same procedure to suggest that the people had nothing to pay this month and ask for a confirmation or correction.

This procedure, which we have called *scheduling,* has been used for all regular income sources and expenditures (Kersten et al., 1990). It considerably reduces the amount of work required of the respondents, especially when combined with the procedure described below.

Grouping in SC Screens. A very simple but efficient way to reduce the amount of work for the respondents is the use of *natural grouping* of items in SC screens. This is especially efficient for regular sources of income and expenditure. By natural grouping, we mean an ordering of the items in such a way that it is immediately clear to the respondents what the researcher wants to know.

If this procedure is combined with scheduling (allowing the respondent to type "0" and press RETURN if nothing has changed), then a long list of boring questions can be answered by one answer and in less than 30 seconds, and the procedure does not reduce the possibilities for indicating changes, because the respondent can correct any number on the screen.

Natural groupings of items can be used for many different topics (e.g., the household-box information, the income of the household, the costs of the house, insurance, membership fees, etc.). When the amounts obtained or spent do not change much through time, these procedures are very efficient and time-saving. If there are considerable changes in these amounts, there is no great advantage to be obtained using these methods, but they will certainly not increase the amount of work.

Some General Comments. Summarizing the above-specified options, panel research allows all the possibilities for improving data quality mentioned before.

The amount of possibilities depends on whether the procedure is interviewer-administered or self-administered. In this section, to the possibilities discussed earlier have been added procedures that are only possible in panel research. We have mentioned several procedures that prevent or detect errors in data and allow for corrections in panel research. These procedures directly improve the data collection: In this connection, we discussed dynamic range checks, dynamic SC screens, and the use of a dynamic calendar. Besides that, we discussed several procedures for reducing the amount of work required of the respondents. These procedures do not directly lead to improvements in the data, but we would nevertheless expect a positive effect on the data quality due to the lesser burden on the respondents.

One point we have not yet mentioned is that the scheduling procedures also have the advantage of reminding the respondent very explicitly of a number of items that have to be mentioned. In this way, scheduling is a very attractive way of aiding the memory of the respondents. In this respect, these procedures are similar to what is known in the literature as *bounded recall,* where people are reminded of what they said last time in order to get better data this time (Neter and Waksberg, 1963, 1964, 1965). In our approach, this possibility is extended to offer memory support over much longer periods, because it is not necessarily the last answer that is mentioned, but the most appropriate answer for a particular point in time.

Of course, there are also disadvantages connected with these procedures. There is the danger of panel effects, but that is not a specific problem for the procedures mentioned here. This is a feature these procedures have in common with all others for panel research. More specific problems are the following: Respondents may have a tendency to indicate no change if this option is made too easy. If scheduling is used, small changes in time, an earlier payment, or a later payment than expected could lead to errors. These errors, however, can be solved relatively easily.

The tendency to indicate no change could be solved in two ways. One is to ask the respondents explicitly to confirm each separate item on the screen, which requires more effort and is not so different from changing a number. A second possibility is to introduce extra questions for those who indicate that no changes have occurred. These questions could appear to be checking why no changes have occurred. If the questions are complex enough and time-consuming enough to balance the two options, the respondents will not make unjustified use of the no-change option in the future. Further research on this point is necessary.

The second problem, of deviations from the expected schedule in periodic activities, can be counteracted by asking extra questions. For example, in a questionnaire asking about different periodic expenditures using a scheduling system, deviations from the scheduling can be counteracted by producing a screen specifying all relevant items where no payment is made, as follows:

Is it correct that you did not make any payment for the following items last month?
___
___

The lines refer to the different expenditures that were expected to be zero according to the scheduling system. The advantage of this procedure is that one can be more sure about the correctness of the data. On the other hand, it is more work for the respondents. Further research is required on this point as well.

For a delay in payment, the solution is much simpler. In that case the information that no payment was made or received is stored to be used in the next interview. In the next month's interview, the same question is asked again. This procedure is used for a number of income sources in questionnaires designed for income and expenditure by Kersten et al. (1990).

This section has shown that computer-assisted panel research has even more possibilities for improving data than the same procedures in cross-sectional research, but one has to check the questionnaires very carefully. Without good questionnaire-checking procedures, there is a serious danger that the complex questionnaires themselves are going to produce errors, due to errors in the programs. Besides this, the programs can become so complex that one will be very reluctant to ever change the questionnaire, because any change would be very difficult to incorporate. As a consequence, the data collection procedures can become inflexible. Researchers will have to decide in the future which characteristic of the data collection instruments they will give priority to: research flexibility or the quality of the collected data. This point and other points connected with the technical aspects of designing CADAC questionnaires are the topic of Chapter 3.

3. WRITING QUESTIONNAIRES

In the first two chapters, we have tried to impress on the reader that designing CADAC questionnaires requires not only the commonly recognized skills for writing questionnaires, as discussed in many textbooks, but also some new skills related to the new possibilities of CADAC. In the past, many designers of programs for CADAC, myself included, have tried to make the point that for their program the questionnaire designer only needs the skills needed to design paper-and-pencil questionnaires. This is indeed true for certain programs, if one does not design complex questionnaires and if one does not use all the possibilities of the systems.

House (1985), Nicholls and House (1987), and House and Nicholls (1988) have argued very convincingly that CATI instruments should be treated not only as survey questionnaires but also as computer programs. Their arguments should be extended to any type of CADAC instrument. Therefore, it is also necessary in this monograph to discuss the programming aspects of these procedures. Because House and Nicholls have made a considerable effort to clarify this point, we will rely in this chapter very much on their contribution, but will generalize their arguments to any type of computer-assisted data collection system.

Looking at the design of questionnaires from a programming point of view, it seems reasonable that the instruments should satisfy the following requirements:

The first and most obvious requirement is that the questionnaire should be able to collect the information for which it has been designed, under all circumstances. Nicholls and House have paid a lot of attention in their papers to the fact that questionnaires should produce correct results not only under normal circumstances, going forward in the questionnaire, but also if one goes back in the questionnaire to change some answers, or if one takes any other action that the system permits. It requires a lot of effort to check whether a program is correct under normal conditions, let alone to check whether programs work correctly under all circumstances.

Second, the instruments should be designed in such a way that it is not too difficult to change the questionnaire for future use. This requirement is not automatically satisfied. Questionnaires can be so complex, as we have mentioned before, that researchers will be very reluctant to change them for fear that the first requirement of correctness will not be satisfied anymore. If the use of CADAC instruments were to result in inflexible questionnaire design, this would be a very bad consequence. Therefore, extra attention should be paid to this point in the design stage.

The third requirement House and Nicholls (1988) have drawn attention to is the *portability* of questionnaires. By portability, they mean that it should be easy to use the same questionnaire or parts of a questionnaire in different studies without the risk of getting a lot of errors. It is, of course, always possible to adjust a new questionnaire till it satisfies the first criterion mentioned above, but it is better to take portability into account during the actual design of the questionnaire, so that one does not need so much time for testing.

The last point we would like to mention is the requirement for questionnaires to be designed in such a way that not only the first author but also other people can change the questionnaire and use it in different contexts. If this requirement is not satisfied, the effort put into the design of a complex questionnaire cannot be fully exploited. Given the mobility of highly qualified people, even the best questionnaires will have a short life if this requirement is not taken very seriously.

In order to satisfy these requirements, one has to take them into account in the process of designing questionnaires. We will make some general remarks about what this means for the design of instruments first, and then in the rest of this chapter we will try to make some suggestions for structuring the design process so that these rules are taken into account.

Starting with the first requirement, it will be clear that a lot of testing is needed before one can be sure that the questionnaire program satisfies this requirement. These tests can be divided into three subtests. The first is the test of the syntax of the questionnaire, the second is the test of the branching and skipping procedures, and the third is the test of correct interpretation by respondents. The first two types of tests evaluate quite different aspects of the questionnaire. Even if the syntax of a questionnaire is correct, this does not guarantee at all that the appropriate information will be collected.

These two types of tests are only sufficient for testing the correctness of the code. They do not guarantee that the questions will be correctly interpreted by respondents. This aspect of the correctness requires field tests in small pilot studies.

However, syntactic and semantic correctness and validity do not guarantee correctness under all circumstances (e.g., under conditions of backing up and making corrections). Nicholls and House (1987) have correctly stressed this point, arguing that programs should be designed in such a way that no errors result from such moves. We will return to this important point in the next chapter. In this chapter, we will concentrate on the other tests to satisfy the requirement of correctness of the questionnaire.

The second important requirement mentioned was flexibility, so that the questionnaires can be changed. This requirement can be satisfied if the questionnaire is designed in such a way that the effects of changes in the questionnaire are limited in scope. In other words, it should be easy to determine what part of the program will be affected by any change. In computer programming, modular design is used for this purpose. This means that one "decomposes" the total task of the program into subtasks and then subdivides these further, until one reaches a very elementary level of sub-routines that can exist independently of each other, and therefore can be designed and tested independently of the other parts of the program. These independent parts, which we call *modules*, can be changed without affecting the other parts of the program as long as the input and output remain the same. From a CADAC point of view, groups of questions concerned with a similar topic should be grouped in such modules. By doing so, changes can be introduced into modules without affecting other parts of the questionnaire. In this way, future changes in the questionnaire are already taken into account in the design.

The use of modules also can be very helpful in making the questionnaire, or parts of it, portable. Given that the modules are clearly defined with respect to their input, output and function, they can be easily implemented in other questionnaires as well. So the modular design also satisfies the third require-ment. It is then possible to make a kind of "library" of modules that can be combined to formulate questionnaires for different studies.

Finally, the use of a clear design using modules helps to make it possible for different people to understand the same questionnaire. But normally this is not enough. Often the designs still can be so difficult that a second researcher will be afraid to look into somebody else's program. In order to avoid this as far as possible, one should add to the modular design a good documentation of each module. This should be done both on paper and in the questionnaire, if the CADAC program allows such comments.

Often the documentation is left till last, and it is common practice not to do it at all. This common practice has a devastating effect on the life span of questionnaires. Therefore, the documentation should be taken up during the design of the questionnaire. This has the further advantage that it also simpli-fies communication. We will come back to this point later.

These considerations have led to the formulation of the following impor-tant steps, which should be taken into consideration during the design of a questionnaire:

1. Start by decomposing the research problem into smaller tasks that can be studied independently of all other parts. If these smaller tasks, or modules, are con-nected to each other, indicate the order in which they should be performed.
2. Design the procedure to be used for each module, using flow charts to document the program.
3. Specify the questionnaire, the input and output variables needed in the module, the criterion values used for checks and branchings that might be variable through time, and the responses that will be produced.

4. Test the syntax and semantics of each module and the combination of modules.

5. Do a field test with the questionnaire in the presence of an interviewer in order to establish whether the respondents understand the questions in the way they are supposed to be understood.

6. Check if the program generates the data that are needed, for the statistical analysis.

Only after all these steps have been carried out successfully can one have some assurance that the questionnaire satisfies the above specified criteria with respect to quality, flexibility, portability, and understandability. It also means that one can be reasonably sure that the instrument will work without too many problems and that the data will satisfy the data requirements.

In the next section, we will say a few more words about each of these steps in the design process and illustrate the procedure with an example. The example that will be used is a questionnaire designed by Kersten et al. (1990) for family income and expenditure surveys, designed for a completely automatic panel study.

The Modularization of the Questionnaire

Most of the time, questionnaires are too complex to be designed as a whole. It is better to divide the questionnaire into parts that perform different tasks. In order to arrive at the level of manageable modules, one sometimes has to decompose the different parts several times.

In the income and expenditure survey mentioned above, four different parts were distinguished, and then the expenditure questionnaire was again split into two parts: one part for regular expenditure and one for incidental expenditure. This decomposition process led to the following five quite independent modules.

- The household box
- The special-events box
- The income box
- Regular-expenditure box
- The incidental-expenditure box

The first two questionnaires were planned to provide the background information needed in the other three questionnaires to reduce the size of the questionnaires for the respondents.

The household box asks for all necessary information about the household composition. This information plays a role in the questions about income; for example, children under 12 will not be asked about their work. Note that the household box provides information for the income box but not vice versa; the questionnaires need to be presented in a specific order, but they can be developed independently.

In the special-events box, information about the house and any illnesses in the last month is asked for. This information is needed from all household members, so the household box must be filled in before the special-events questionnaire. The information from the latter questionnaire then is used in the questionnaire about expenditure.

The use of information from one questionnaire in another determines the sequence of the questionnaires, as indicated in Figure 3.1. The sequence is indicated by the direction of the arrows. The figure shows that the questionnaires have to be done in sequence, going from the top (the household box) to the bottom (the regular expenditure box).

Figure 3.1 also indicates that each questionnaire has its own information source that is used after the first interview, called a *matrix*. These matrices are intended to be used for presentation in the dynamic SC screens in order to update the information on the specific topic. This example shows quite clearly how the decomposition of the questionnaire into modules can be represented. A rather complex questionnaire is presented here in a very simple way. Once this picture is understood, each individual module can be considered without worrying about the other modules in the questionnaire. This is precisely the reason for decomposing the questionnaire.

Design of the Modules

Before the questionnaire is written in detail, it always makes sense to make a flow chart of the questionnaire to be developed. In doing so, the problems of the questionnaire will become clear and one can look for solutions by improving the flow chart. Different rules for the formulation of flow charts are used in practice (Jabine, 1985). The rules we have used are indicated in the flow chart of the household box, presented in Figure 3.2.

In Figure 3.2, the following rules have been applied:

1. Procedures that indicate decisions by the program have been indicated by diamonds; for example, if it is the first interview, the program follows the scheme on the right, and if it is a subsequent interview the program starts on the left.

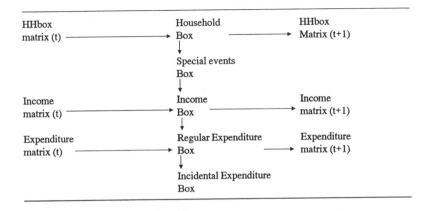

Figure 3.1. The Structure of an Income and Expenditure Questionnaire

2. Questions to which the responses determine the further procedures are presented in screens with the question text. For example, the question "How many people are living in the household?" determines later on how many questions have to be asked about names, birthdays, and so on.

3. Elaborate procedures containing sets of questions concerning factual information are presented in boxes, and the topics are indicated with bold letters. We call these procedures *question procedures.*

4. SC screens are presented by a combination of a screen and a question. For example, there is an SC screen with the text:

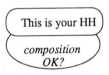

The top part indicates that an SC screen is presented and the bottom part shows the question presented on the screen.

5. Arrows indicate the direction in which the process goes. A double headed arrow indicates that the process can go back and forth. For example, if the names are incorrect, the program goes to the procedure "correct names." There the correct names are requested. Then the result is again presented and checked by the respondent. If there is still an error, further corrections can be made, and so on.

66

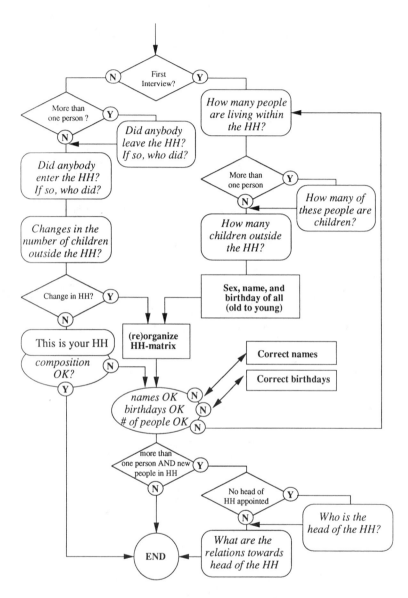

Figure 3.2. The Flow Chart of the Household Box Information

It should be mentioned that range checks and consistency checks are not indicated in this figure. For most of the questions, checks could be specified: Loops and question procedures should be indicated for all questions, but this would take too much space and would be more confusing than clarifying. Therefore, the checks are not indicated in the flow chart.

Having described the form of presentation used in the flow charts, we can now describe the basic characteristics of the household-box questionnaire as presented here.

First of all, a distinction is made as to whether it is the first interview or not. If it is the first interview, all the basic information has to be collected as indicated on the right-hand side of Figure 3.2. Once all the necessary information has been collected, an SC screen is presented to ask the respondent to check the correctness of the information. If errors are present, corrections can be made until all information is correct according to the respondent. Finally a "head of the household" is chosen. When this choice has been made, the questionnaire asks the relationship of all persons in the household to the head of this household. After these questions the process is finished and the next interview can start.

If the respondent has to fill in this questionnaire again, the procedure is normally much simpler because most of the information concerning names, gender, ages, and so forth remains the same. The only possible changes are that someone has left the household or has come into the household.

If nothing has changed, the respondent goes immediately to the SC screen that provides all the information about the household and asks whether the composition is still the same. If that is the case, this questionnaire is finished and new interviews can be carried out. If changes have occurred, minor corrections have to be specified, the SC screen is again shown, and then the questionnaire is finished. The use of the SC screen in this case is clearly very efficient and saves a lot of time and effort.

This illustration indicates very well the usefulness of the flow charts. It is a handy tool for the design of questionnaires. It also facilitates discussions with clients and other designers of questionnaires about the structure of the questionnaire.

On the other hand, the design is still not complete with the design of the flow chart. Often, the final formulation of the questionnaire is a creative process that can change the flow chart. The design of a flow chart, however, is a useful tool not only for communication between researchers but also as documentation for later use.

Specification of the Questionnaire

The next step is the specification of the questionnaire itself. Although the flow chart specifies in considerable detail what should be written in the questionnaire, the flow chart is still program independent and easily understood. The text written for different CADAC programs starting with the same flow chart can be very different. Also, the way the text will be produced is very different: Some remarks on this point will be made in the next chapter. Here we will concentrate on the more general aspect of the specification of the questionnaire. Having specified the flow chart, the following steps still must be taken.

- Edit the questions in sequence and in the appropriate syntax
- Specify the branching and skipping
- Specify any procedures not yet specified
- Specify consistency checks and the extra questions necessary for this purpose
- Specify the information saved and stored for later use
- Specify the responses to be stored in the data file

In this process, so many new components will be added to the questionnaire that it is necessary for documentation purposes to provide additional information (besides the flow chart) in order to make the questionnaire understandable to other people. One way to do this is to provide a paper version of the questionnaire text as well as the computer version of it. In itself, however, this is not enough. It is very useful to do the following.

- Place comments in the questionnaire text, if possible
- Provide an overview of the different variables that are used in the module

An illustration of the first recommendation would be to write in the questionnaire text "The procedure CORRECT NAMES starts here" or "Variable V1 contains the age of the respondent" or "Consistency check of the age and relationship with the head of the household." The structure of the questionnaire is much easier to understand with the help of such comments.

The second point mentioned concerns the specification of variables. The specification of the variables has two purposes. The first purpose is to indicate what values have been chosen for the constants used in the questionnaire. Criteria for consistency checks are relatively arbitrary. For example, a clarifying question can be asked when the father is 50 years older than his presumed daughter or when the age difference is only 13 years. However, these criteria are arbitrary. In order to indicate which criteria are used and to be able to correct them in all places where they are used simultaneously, one can start the interview with a specification of the values of these constants by writing (for example)

V60=50 \ the upper limit for a father-daughter age difference\
V61=13 \ the lower limit for a father-daughter age difference\

In the questionnaire, the check now is written as

If (age>v60) or (age<v61) then . . .

If in a later study these limits need to be changed, they can be changed on the first page of the questionnaire, and this change automatically will be taken into account at all places in the questionnaire where V60 or V61 is used. This procedure will prevent programming errors that occur when a correction is forgotten.

The second purpose of the specification of the variables is to indicate explicitly the relationship between the module and other parts of the questionnaire. The other parts can only communicate with the module in question by providing information about values of input variables or by using the values of the output variables obtained from the relevant module. In the case of the household box, the input and output variables are the same. These variables, for all members of the household, are membership number, gender, year of birth, day of birth, relationship with the head of the household, membership number of last month, and the name of the respondent. This information is summarized in Table 3.1. The household box module uses this information for specification of the SC screens of the next month (input); the same variables also are produced by this module as output variables each month, and these values will be used in other modules to reduce the number of questions in them.

Finally, it is useful to make a list for each module of the responses that are returned to the researcher for further analysis. It is possible that not all answers will be of interest to the researcher; for example, if consistency checks are made, the incorrect answers do not have to be returned. In this case it should be clear which answers are to be returned and which are not. This information is important if one has to check whether the appropriate information is provided by the questionnaire.

TABLE 3.1
The Variables Used in the Household Box

Member	1	2	3	4	5	6	7	8	9
Member # last month	V11	V12	V13	V14	V15	V16	V17	V18	V19
Gender	V21	V22	V23	V24	V25	V26	V27	V28	V29
Year of birth	V31	V32	V33	V34	V35	V36	V37	V38	V39
Month of birth	V41	V42	V43	V44	V45	V46	V47	V48	V49
Day of birth	V51	V52	V53	V54	V55	V56	V57	V58	V59
Relationship with head	V61	V62	V63	V64	V65	V66	V67	V68	V69
Name	X11	X12	X13	X14	X15	X16	X17	X18	X19

The writing of the questionnaire is only a part of the task that must be performed. It should be kept in mind that the documentation is at least as important if one would like to use a specific questionnaire more than once.

Testing the Syntax and Branching

Any new questionnaire will contain some errors. These errors can be of different natures. One of the most difficult type of errors to avoid is the syntax error. By a syntax error, we mean that text is made that is not in agreement with the grammar used in the CADAC program. Such errors can lead to many problems if the program does not provide tools to detect them. The errors could appear very minor to the questionnaire constructor, but an omitted bracket or a comma instead of a period can interrupt the program, and the error can be very hard to detect.

In order to prevent such errors, some CADAC programs provide menu-driven questionnaire writing facilities. This makes it impossible to make syntactical errors. On the other hand, such programs often are not very sophisticated in their possible applications.

Other programs provide what amounts to a computer language to write questionnaires. The written code is compiled to make a questionnaire program. These programs normally have a facility in the compilation stage to indicate where a syntactical error has been found in the program.

Finally, there are CADAC programs that require the designer of the questionnaire to add some instructions for the program to a normal questionnaire. The INTERV program used in this monograph is an example of this type. Programs of this kind interpret the written text and present the different pieces of information on the screen. They normally do not have syntax-checking facilities. If there is an error, one will discover it while doing the interview, when the program ends in an error or does not present the correct questions and answer categories on the screen. Although these programs have the advantage that they do not require compilation, which means that the questionnaire can be used immediately, their disadvantage is that they do not indicate syntax errors. In the case of the INTERV program, this problem has been solved by developing another program (SYSFILE) that checks the syntax, among other things.

We cannot generalize much about these specific checking procedures, because they are very program-dependent. There is one general remark, however, that should be made on this point. Above, we have stressed the importance of modular design, partly with the testing problems in mind. It is of the utmost importance in the construction of complex questionnaires that they be tested at the modular level first. This makes the detection and correction of errors more simple and manageable. If one is testing large questionnaires, a diagnostic often is not very helpful, because it might be due to an error at a different point in the text. Also, the effect of changes at the modular level is very limited for the whole program, so the changes are also of restricted magnitude.

Only after all modules have been tested and shown to be correct, can one start testing the combination of modules. If an error is detected in a combination of modules that already have been tested, the error must lie in the connection between the modules. Thus, the modular construction also helps in the diagnostics.

Concerning the testing of the branching and skipping patterns in a questionnaire, the same argument holds: It is better to start by testing the modules before testing the whole questionnaire. In fact, it is even more necessary in this case, because there are as yet no formal tools available to check the validity of the branching and skipping specifications, although some theoretical work has begun in this field (Willenborg, 1989). Obvious errors that can be spotted very easily are (a) questions that cannot be reached from any other question, due to incorrect specification of a question name; and (b) branching that leads to the end of the questionnaire.

Such problems can even be indicated by a program; for example, the above mentioned program SYSFILE has these possibilities for questionnaires written for INTERV. But even in these cases, the programs cannot indicate where errors have been made in the branching and skipping specifications. This can only be determined by the researchers.

There are also many branchings that are correct from a syntactical point of view, but wrong from a theoretical point of view. In trying out a questionnaire, these errors will be detected if the order of the questions leads to very strange combinations. But the questionnaire also can look normal and nevertheless be wrong. If one does not have special tools, it can take a lot of time to detect these errors in a complex questionnaire, and one needs to have a very clear idea of what should happen in the questionnaire.

Programs could provide interpretations of the branching and skipping specifications in tree structures or other forms. If such presentations are compact and clear, they can provide a lot of help in the detection of errors. The development of such programs should be a top priority of survey-research programmers, because they would be very useful tools. Without these programs, one has to rely on manual checking of the questionnaires. This is a very time-consuming but nevertheless necessary task in all CADAC studies.

Testing Questionnaires in Pilot Studies

As we have already mentioned, the syntactical correctness and the validity of the branching and skipping specifications do not mean that the questionnaire will work properly. It is our experience, and the experience of many survey researchers, that carefully chosen text can be misinterpreted by respondents in many different ways.

For this reason, it is absolutely essential to test any CADAC instrument in the field in small pilot projects before it is used in a large survey. It is common practice to carry these tests out in two stages. The first test is done in the institute by other survey researchers, on the basis that a group always knows more than an individual. This is certainly a necessary step, but it is not sufficient to be sure of the correct interpretation. A second test then is done in a small field study, and should be carried out by interviewers even if the questionnaire is a self-administered questionnaire. In the latter case, the interviewer should not read the questions but only listen to the remarks the respondents are making or the clarifying questions they ask. Our department (University of Amsterdam, Methodology Department) normally uses 30 to 50 interviews to test questionnaires. The amount depends on whether new errors still are being reported by the interviewers.

The problems that are reported will lead to the reformulation of questions and to the introduction of help screens where necessary, or even to complete changes in the questionnaire design. If there are many problems reported, it might be necessary to do a second pilot study. This was the case in the design of a CADAC questionnaire for time-budget research that led to many problems in a first pilot study (Kalfs, 1986).

If one has several alternative formulations for the same questions and one does not know which to chose, CADAC has the attractive feature that split-ballot experiments can be designed very easily if one has the facility of a random generator in the program. In that case, one can randomly determine which respondent gets which form of the questionnaire and determine afterwards which form was more successful. This experimental work within a questionnaire has been discussed recently in the literature (Shanks, 1989), but these possibilities have been available for a long time.

Recently, the discussion between cognitive psychologists and survey researchers has led to cognitive analyses of the tasks that survey researchers set their respondents. These studies now are providing new suggestions for experiments with different formulations of tasks that should be experimented with (see, e.g., Blair and Burton, 1986; Silberstein, 1989). CADAC provides good facilities for these purposes.

The work of Belson (1981) has made it very clear that this kind of testing should be done. He even recommends in-depth interviews to find out how the questions are interpreted. Although his point is clear, one does not usually have the time or money for such experiments. But in the case of a long-term study that uses the same questionnaire over and over again, it is certainly recommended to consider this possibility before the definite questionnaire is chosen.

As a weak substitute for Belson's recommendation, we provide the respondents in our self-administered CADAC questionnaires with one page for comments on our questions after each module. Most of the time, the respondents report errors they have made, which provides us with valuable information about problems that occur in the questionnaire, but sometimes they clearly indicate problems they have had with the questions. In this way, information is obtained that can help us to improve data collection instruments.

Our general impression is that this phase does not get enough attention in practical research. Researchers normally assume too quickly that their interpretation of questions is the same as the interpretation by the respondents. For a more elaborate discussion of the design of field tests, see Nelson (1985).

Testing the Data

The last test to be performed before the instrument can be used in practice is a test of the data produced by the CADAC instrument. As we mentioned earlier, it is possible that some answers (later on corrected) are not stored in the data file. But if such an option is provided by a program, it is also possible to make errors. If the specification for the deletion of an answer is given for the wrong question, one will not get the data one needs in the statistical analysis. Such errors, if they are not detected, can completely ruin a study, as the necessary data can never be recovered (unlike in paper questionnaires), because the data are omitted during the data collection and not stored. One suggestion would be to store all information, but sometimes the number of variables is so large that one has to reduce this quantity to be able to analyze the data efficiently.

Many CADAC programs are able to generate a system file for different statistical packages. Such programs use the specified questionnaire to generate an input for the job to make a system file. In such a job, all the information about the variable names and variable labels is mentioned, and such a text can be used to check the correctness and completeness of the data file generated by the questionnaire. If errors exist in this structure, one can still make the changes; if one has finished the data collection it is too late.

This is also a good place to mention that the above specified programs or subroutines are a very attractive component of the CADAC procedures. Not having to make the system files manually saves the researcher a lot of time. In the past, this job could easily take 3 days or more. Using these programs, this task can be done in a few minutes, so it is possible to start the data analysis within a few minutes after the data collection has been finished.

Nevertheless, with respect to the testing of the data structure, we would recommend that such a check on the correctness and completeness of the data file is always done before the data collection. Only when this last test has been done can one start the data collection with some confidence in the whole process.

4. CADAC HARDWARE AND SOFTWARE

It would be impossible here to give an overview of all existing hardware and software for computer-assisted data collection, nor is that the purpose of this chapter. What we can do in this chapter is provide the reader with the information that will help to make the important choices when choosing a system. On this point, there is very little systematic information, and there are many different systems available. The information that is available is mainly directed at the evaluation of CATI systems. In this chapter, we will put forward a more general approach that takes into account the various possible applications discussed above. Perhaps we can provide some insight into this jungle of computer programs by discussing some of the hardware and software choices that are relevant for the user. Let us start with the hardware.

CADAC Hardware

With CADAC hardware, there are two major issues at stake. The first concerns the choice of a computer system, the second has to do with the choice of a communication system. The issues are connected, but they can be discussed separately. Of course, the major issue is the choice of computer system, so we will start with this point.

From Mini- to PC-Based Systems. Computer-assisted data collection started with CATI systems that were designed for mainframe or minicomputers connected by direct lines with terminals (Dutka and Frankel, 1980; Fink, 1983). All the processing is done on the central computer; the terminals present only the results of this processing and receive the keyed answers. Such a system is efficient for CATI systems if all the interviewers are working in a room close to the computer, but it is not suitable for other applications discussed in this text like CAPI and CAPAR.

Although terminals connected through modems to central computers could have been used in other applications, this has not in fact happened. Experiments with computer-assisted interviewing on PCs have been going on since 1980 (Danielsson and Maarstad, 1982; Palit and Sharp, 1983; Saris, de Pijper and Neijens, 1982). PCs are more flexible, because they can function independently of a central computer. Given their improved portability, PCs can be used for personal interviewing as well as for CATI and CAPAR. Because many special interest groups among respondents, such as doctors or business people, have a PC at home, these systems can also be used for compuer assisted mail interviews or CAMI.

The major advantage of using a PC- (especially an MS.DOS) based system for CADAC, besides reduction of costs, is that the same interview program can be used for all the different applications mentioned. This means that the research staff need only become familiar with one program for data collection, and the data collection can be done in many different ways. In the previous chapter, we mentioned that programs that can be used for self-administered CADAC interviews can be used for all other applications. This is not the case for the older mini-based systems. Some of these older systems are now also available in PC-based versions, because of the wider range of applications of PC-based systems.

Some organizations claim that this wide range of applications is a special feature of their system. We hope that we have made it clear here that this is nothing special for a PC-based system, because all PC-based systems have this potential. The versatility of a PC-based system depends on the amount of effort put into developing a good communication and management system for the different applications.

Having expressed a preference for PC-based systems for their wide range of possible applications, and for MS.DOS systems because of their widespread use, we now come to the next choice: the communication system. (First, however, we should stress that this preference for PC-based systems does not mean that mini-based systems do not have their value for CATI applications. There are some very sophisticated mini-based CATI systems that certainly can compete with PC-based systems for the same application. If one chooses such a system, however, one should be aware that it will probably be necessary to learn a different program if one also would like to use CADAC for other applications.)

Communication Systems for CADAC. Choosing a PC-based system does not limit the choice of communication system or the choice of central computer. In principle, four different procedures can be used.

- A stand-alone or mail-based system
- A wide area modem-based system
- A local area network (LAN)
- Direct lines between the PC and the central computer

The most elementary use of a PC-based system is as a "stand-alone" computer, to collect the data with no need for contact with a central computer. In that case, the program, administration, and interviews can simply be mailed, or handed over to the interviewer if the data collection occurs close to the research center. When the interviews are finished, the diskette is returned, and the results are stored in a central computer for analysis. In this way, no communication system is needed. Such a system is very cheap, but it can be used only on a very small scale. Above approximately 10 stand-alone computers, such a system becomes unreliable, because one easily can make mistakes when handling the data on the diskettes. On the other hand, it is definitely the cheapest form in which CADAC systems can be used.

The second system, the wide area modem-based system, is especially useful for CAPI and CAPAR applications. Information can be exchanged through modems and telephone lines with computers at a distance via the RS232 connector on the PC. This kind of system allows interviews and administration to be sent over the telephone line from a central computer to the remote PC of an interviewer or household. The interview then can be carried out on the remote PC because the computer can function on its own. In this way, interviews can be carried out independent of and very far from the central computer. This system is efficient for CAPI and CAPAR, especially tele-interviewing, but also can be used for decentralized CATI applications. For centralized CATI applications such a system is not recommended, because over small distances it is better to use local area networks. If long distance telephone calls are very expensive in a particular country, however, it would make sense to consider a decentralized modem-based CATI system.

In the future these systems will no longer require modems, when the new ISDN standard is introduced for telephone and datalines. Communication then will also be much faster. This is especially attractive for transmitting pictures over long distances, which now takes a long time and is therefore rather expensive. For more details on these developments and their consequences, see Gonzalez (1990).

The third possibility, the local area network (LAN), has been developed for centralized CATI systems. In this system, the computers are connected to a server (a stronger PC) by special cards and coaxial cables, allowing fast communication between computers over small distances. In a LANs, the PCs can work alone, but still obtain and provide information fairly frequently from or to a server through the network. The very fact that this system is called a "local area network" indicates that this system is especially useful for CATI applications, although because LAN can be used to connect remote PCs nowadays, it can also be used for CAPI, CAPAR, or CAMI. The information exchanged in the system between the PCs and the server can vary. The frequency of contact and the amount of information transmitted each time depends on the management program used. For example, one may give an interviewer a set of names and numbers of people to be called and return all information only after the whole list has been done. It is also possible for the server to keep complete control over the whole process, so that contact with the server is made by the PC each time a task has been completed. Depending on the management system used, the PCs can work more or less independent of the server.

Finally, the old mini-based system can be simulated by using the PCs as terminals connected to a central computer. This kind of system, where the PCs do not function on their own but are only used as screens to convey messages between the PCs and the central computer, only makes sense for centralized CATI applications and cannot be used for any other application. This system would appear outdated nowadays, because it ignores one of the important advantages of the PC, namely, that it can function on its own as a data collection system. To use a different data collection system one has to rewrite the whole interview program.

It should be clear from this discussion that systems that can use PCs as stand-alone computers are very attractive, because they can be used for many different applications. This is especially true for the first three options, although the first option is only reasonable if one wishes to test the possibilities of such systems. The most serious candidates for practical research are the wide area modem-based system and the LAN-based system. These also can be used next to each other. They have different applications that require different management systems, but the interview program can remain the same. Whether the different programs provide the facilities for the different applications depends on the company and the amount of effort put into developing the management systems. Therefore, there is no reason to prefer one over the other as far as the scale of possible applications is concerned. The choice should be based on the planned application and the potential of the software under consideration.

CADAC Software

Besides the choice of hardware, the choice of software must be made. These two choices are not independent of each other. Most of the time the software is provided for a specific hardware system (i.e., stand-alone computers, a LAN-based system, or a modem-based system, or combinations of these systems). Therefore, the next question is "What are the requirements for the software?" This question has been answered unanimously for CATI systems (Baker and Lefes, 1988; Nicholls, 1988; Nicholls and Groves, 1986). The functional requirements can be generalized to other CADAC applications quite easily. In doing so, the following requirements for the software can be specified:

1. The sample management should be done by the system and not by the researcher.
2. The contacts between interviewers and respondents or the selection of interviews for the household members should be scheduled by the program.
3. On-line interviewing should be arranged by the program.
4. The quality and quantity of the work of the interviewers should be controlled by the system.
5. The system should produce more or less automatically the data files for statistical analysis.

We would like to add to this list a sixth requirement:

6. The questionnaire authoring system should not be too difficult to use and should provide sufficient flexibility and testing facilities.

We will now make some brief comments on each of these requirements.

Sample Management. Even when the population from which the sample is drawn is the same, the sample frame used for different CADAC applications can be quite different. For CATI, one could use telephone directories or random-digit dialing methods, whereas for CAPI, lists of addresses are the most obvious source of information. But whatever the sample frame, a program should be able to draw a sample from a list of cases provided to the program. Furthermore, the program should be able to keep track of the results of the data collection: whether a household has been contacted; if so, what the result of this contact was, or why the household refuses to cooperate, and so forth. All this information should be organized by the program. If it has to be done on paper by the researcher, it requires a lot of work and this can lead to errors and arbitrary decisions. This has been shown convincingly by Palit and Sharp (1983). Imagine that one wishes to interview people with a specific characteristic that occurs in only 10% of households, and one would like to talk to 1,000 people with this characteristic. Then 10,000 calls are needed to find these 1,000 people. If random dialing is used, with a success rate of 30% one must manipulate 30,000 records to realize these 1,000 interviews. This example illustrates the necessity of a computer-based management system in the central computer.

Scheduling of Contacts. In each application, different procedures are used to select, administer, and schedule contacts. In CATI systems, the combination of interviewer and telephone number has to be selected, and a schedule for the calls has to be designed. In CAPI applications, interviewers and addresses have to be selected, and a sequence of visits has to be determined. But in tele-interviewing, the computer only has to make a combination of interviews and household members if not all members get the same interviews.

In all applications, the status of the work has to be administered, and decisions have to be made about what the next step in the process should be. All these tasks can be done better by the computer than by human beings, if the program works well. This does not mean that the computer program can do all the work. There are still a large number of decisions that researchers have to make.

Although these management programs are similar with respect to their tasks, they will be sufficiently different to require different modules depending on the application used. Often, not all modules are available in all programs: The programs are often specialized to one application.

Programs also will be different in the way they organize these tasks. Some programs (CATI-oriented systems) will organize these tasks mainly on the central computer. Programs more oriented toward CAPI and CAPAR will organize these tasks mainly on the PCs, which has the advantage that the systems can continue to function if the network fails. This is not the case with the other systems, which are more dependent on the central computer.

On-Line Interviewing. In earlier texts on CATI procedures, the following necessary characteristics of CATI systems have been mentioned (Nicholls, 1988; Nicholls and Groves, 1986):

1. The system displays instructions, survey questions, and response categories on the computer screen.
2. Screens may contain "fills" or alterations of the display text based on prior answers or batch input from case records.
3. Answers to closed questions may be numeric or alphanumeric codes; and these codes and other numeric entries may be edited by sets of permissible values, by ranges, or by logical or arithmetic operations.
4. Edit failures may result either in an unaccepted entry (requiring another attempt) or in the display of additional probes or questions to be asked.
5. Extended text answers may be entered for open questions.
6. Branching or skipping to the next item is automatic and may be based on logical or arithmetic tests of any prior entries or input data.

7. Interviewers and respondents may interrupt and resume interviews in mid-course; review, back up to, and (if permitted) change prior entries; and enter interviewing notes at appropriate points.

These characteristics can be generalized quite easily to any kind of CADAC system, but they give only the minimum requirements for these programs. There are two very elaborate evaluations of computer programs for CADAC of which we are aware. These evaluations (Carpenter, 1988; de Bie et al., 1989) provide many more criteria and an evaluation of programs on the basis of these criteria. They evaluate criteria such as the number of question types, randomization of questions and response categories, and facilities for high-lighting. They also mention more detailed criteria, such as the procedures for skipping and branching (*if, then, else*), and many other possibilities. However, this is not the place to discuss all these criteria; besides, these programs change rather quickly and the state of the art has changed considerably in the last 2 years. Nevertheless, these evaluations also show that the most elaborate systems have most of the important features mentioned. These reports are mainly interesting (we feel) to make readers sensitive to the criteria that they might consider when they have to decide on the purchase of CADAC software. A good example of such a study is that of Connett et al. (1990), who had to make the decision with respect to a new CATI system for the Survey Research Center.

There also are two specialized papers on evaluation research of CAPI systems by Couper and Groves (1989). These papers are especially interesting because they compare the performance of different interfaces between the computer and interviewers. Most common for MS.DOS computers in survey research are menu-driven systems, where the respondent has to type the number of the response category. There are many alternatives, however, that can be considered. The GridPad provides facilities to write answers in uppercase letters in the box provided on the screen. The coding is done by handwriting recognition. The Datellite provides a touch screen, whereby one answers a question by touching the part of the screen where the answer is presented.

In addition to the interfaces studied by Couper and Groves, there is another quite common interface that is also menu driven, but where the answer is chosen by moving the cursor with the cursor keys or a mouse to the appropriate answer. A completely different possibility is the use of bar codes for categories and a bar-code reader for the coding.

Couper and Groves (1989) have made a start with research on the consequences of the choice of the interface for data quality. On the basis of their most recent study, they conclude:

> Both the handwriting recognition and touchscreen machines performed worse than "traditional" laptop computers in terms of speed and certain types of errors. However, such differences could well disappear given sufficient familiarity with and training on these machines. Furthermore, these technologies are still in their relative infancy. It is expected that hardware and software developments (some of which have already been announced) will make these systems easier to use and less error-prone.

Although their results are very interesting, much more research on this point has to be done before it becomes clear which data-entry system is the best for survey research. The conclusion of these studies could well be that the choice should depend on the type and amount of data that is to be collected.

Recently, a distinction was made between different software packages on the basis of another aspect of the use of the screen. It has been suggested that there are item-based, screen-based, and form-based CADAC systems (Nicholls, 1988). *Item-based systems* display one survey question and answer space at a time, perform edits after each entry, and typically erase the screen before the next item appears. *Screen-based systems* present more questions on the screen, but the branching and skipping is still under control of the program. The more recent *form-based systems* provide many questions on the screen, but the interviewer or respondents can move in any direction on the screen and answer the questions in the order they prefer. The edits are done after all questions have been answered.

Although the distinction is very interesting, CADAC systems cannot be characterized so simply on this basis. The systems are adapting so quickly to new demands that systems that were originally item-based now provide facilities that are comparable to those of screen-based and form-based systems. Thus, the systems can not be simply characterized in this way, and the choice should not be based on this feature.

There are other criteria, however, that have not been mentioned yet that deserve more attention. We would like to mention the following criteria.

- The maximum length of the interview
- The facilities to put together complex questionnaires tailor-made for the purpose
- The flexibility of the program for introducing changes into the questionnaire

Some programs limit the length of the questionnaire by the number of questions or by the size of the program that has to be compiled from the interview text. As personalized questionnaires can become very long, this is an important criterion.

The second point stresses an obvious requirement, namely, that one should be able to make the questionnaires one would like to make. Some CADAC programs are very simple to use, but do not provide much flexibility for the design of questionnaires.

The third point relates to a previous discussion, where we argued in favor of programs that allow flexibility in the design and in adjustment of questionnaires. One generally recognized problem in this field concerns the use of numbers for the questions or screens used. If one would like to change a questionnaire, the branching of which is based on numbers, one has to change all the numbers in the questionnaire, and the likelihood of errors in such systems is clearly very high. We will come back to this discussion later. These three points should certainly be taken into account when evaluating good quality CADAC systems.

Quality and Quantity Control. In CATI systems, a distinction is made between quality control by monitoring and control of the quantity of work done by interviewers. The latter task is done by collecting information on the number of calls, outcome of the calls, amount of time spent, productivity, response rate, and so on. In the other applications this distinction cannot be made, but quality controls can still be made by counting the correct codings, the length of the verbal responses, the number of alternatives mentioned in multiple response questions, and so forth.

It is a useful facility if a program can report this information automatically, as some programs do. On the other hand, it is already quite attractive if the information is available and can be evaluated by statistical analysis of the data, which is the case for most programs. Therefore this point does not lead to a very different evaluation of the different programs.

Production of System Files. The production of system files for statistical analysis of the data with one of the commonly used statistical packages, such as SAS, BMDP, SPSS, or any other package, should be a standard facility in any CADAC system. Some packages provide their own statistical package for the CADAC data, but it is difficult to see this as an added attraction, because such a package can never be as complete as the well-known statistical packages. Most of the better CADAC programs, therefore, provide procedures, which on the basis of the information available in the questionnaire, generate system files for different statistical packages.

Although we do not consider this feature of CADAC systems to be an important criterion in the choice of a CADAC system, because all elaborate systems have the facility, we also do not want to underestimate its importance. In the past, the development of a correct input file for constructing a system file could take up to a week. With the automatic procedures available in the CADAC systems, this job is done in a few minutes. This is a very important advantage of CADAC systems.

The Questionnaire-Authoring System. Last but not least, we would like to draw the attention of the reader to the different aspects that are important in the evaluation of the authoring system connected with the CADAC systems.

Some systems seem very attractive because of their simple authoring system, mostly menu-driven. However, these systems are often the least flexible when it comes to designing questionnaires. At the other extreme, there are authoring systems that more or less provide a computer language for writing questionnaires. These systems are certainly very flexible in terms of their possibilities for designing any kind of questionnaire, but one has to be a computer programmer to design such questionnaires, or at least have programmer-like capabilities.

A middle-of-the-road option has been chosen in systems that work on the basis of a program that requires a questionnaire text with extra symbols for the computer. In such systems, like INTERV used in this monograph for illustrative purposes, simple questionnaires can be written very quickly, whereas the possibility to write complex questionnaires depends on the facilities provided by the program. In my experience, the possibilities are as unlimited as in the program-based systems.

A related point is that it should be relatively easy to change a questionnaire if necessary. A typical problem arises when numbers are used for questions or screens, as we have already mentioned. Another point is that it should be possible to develop separate modules that can be combined together in different questionnaires. This facility is provided by most programs. It depends mainly on the author of the questionnaire whether these facilities are properly used (as described in Chapter 3).

One feature that tends to vary quite a lot from one program to another is the very important facility of checking the syntax of a questionnaire and getting some insight into the structure of the branching and skipping patterns specified in the questionnaire. The first facility is very important in helping to avoid wasting a lot of time on very small errors. The programs that provide a kind of computer language to specify questionnaires and that require a compilation stage to produce an interview program from a questionnaire have the advantage of automatically providing an error-detection facility.

Menu-driven authoring programs prevent errors by leaving the authors only limited freedom. But the programs based on interpreters do not normally have error detection facilities. If these facilities do exist in a program, they are developed separately from the interview program. One should take care that such a program is available if one is buying a CADAC system, because it will save the questionnaire authors a lot of time.

An equally attractive feature of a system would be providing tools for representing the branching and skipping in a questionnaire. These specifications can contain many errors, which can cause a lot of problems if not detected by syntax-checking programs. Although these facilities are very important, it will be some time before they will be available on a large scale.

Having discussed the different characteristics that we consider important in the choice of a CADAC system, we also provide a list of CADAC programs in the Appendix for those who are interested in using such a system. It is not possible in this context to offer an evaluation of the different programs (see the evaluations of Carpenter, 1988; Connett et al., 1990; de Bie et al., 1989), but we also should warn the reader that such evaluations are out of date the moment they appear, because the design of CADAC programs is one of the most dynamic fields in computer programming. It is also my conviction that knowledge of the possibilities of these systems is still very limited. We expect that in the near future many new ways will be found to improve computer-assisted data collection. This is one of the reasons why this is such an interesting field of research.

APPENDIX: COMPUTER PROGRAMS FOR CADAC

We provide a list of computer programs for CADAC on PCs without the pretention of completeness and without an evaluation of the quality of the programs. For more information about these programs, see Carpenter (1988), de Bie et al. (1989), and Connett et al. (1990).

ACS Query
Analytical Computer Service, Inc.
640 North Lasalle Drive
Chicago, IL 60610
USA
(312)751-2915

Athena
CRC Information Systems, Inc.
435 Hudson St.
New York, NY 10014
USA
(212) 620-5678

Autoquest
Microtab Systems Pty Ltd.
2 Tanya Way
Eltham, Victoria
3095 Australia
(03)439-6235

Blaise
Central Bureau of Statistics
Hoofdafdeling M3
P. O. Box 959
2270 AZ Voorburg
The Netherlands
(70)694341

CAPPA
The Scientific Press
540 University Ave.
Palo Alto, CA 94301
USA
(415)322-5221

Cases
Computer Assisted Survey Methods
University of California
2538 Channing Way
Berkeley, CA 94720
USA
(415)642-6592

Cass
Survey Research Laboratory
University of Wisconsin
610 Langdon St.
Madison, WI 53703
USA
(608)262-3122

Ci2
Sawtooth Software, Inc.
208 Spruce N.
Ketchum, ID 83340
USA
(208)726-7772

INTERV
Sociometric Research Foundation
Van Boshuizen Str 225
1083 AW Amsterdam
The Netherlands
(020)-6610961

ITS
Information Transfer Systems
2451 S. Industrial Hwy.
Ann Arbor, MI 46104
USA
(313)994-0003

MATI
Social and Economic Sciences
Research Center
Washington State University
Pullman, WA 99164
USA
(509)335-1511

PCRS/ACRS
M/A/R/C Inc.
7850 North Belt Line Rd.
Irving, TX 75063
USA
(214)506-3400

PC-Survent
CfMC, Computers for Marketing
547 Howard St.
San Francisco, CA 94105
USA
(415)777-0470

Quancept
Quantime Limited
17 Bedford Square
London WC1B 3JA
England
(1)6377061

Q-Fast
Statsoft, Inc.
2325 East 13th St.
Tulsa, OK 74104
USA
(918)583-4149

Quester Writer
Orchard Products
205 State Rd.
Princeton, NJ 08540
USA
(609)683-7702

Quiz Whiz
Quiz Whiz Enterprises, Inc.
790 Timberline Dr.
Akron, OH 44304
USA
(216)922-1825

Reach
World Research
P. O. Box 1009
Palatine, IL 60078
USA
(312)911-1122

REFERENCES

ANDREWS, F. M. (1984) "Construct validity and error components of survey measures: A structural modeling approach." *Public Opinion Quarterly* 48: 409-442.

BAKER, R. P., and LEFES, W. L. (1988) "The design of CATI systems: A review of current practice," in R. M. Groves, P. P. Biemer, L. E. Lyberg, J. T. Massey, W. L. Nicholls II, and J. Waksberg (eds.) *Telephone Survey Methodology* (pp. 387-403). New York: John Wiley.

BATISTA, J. M., and SARIS, W. E. (1988) "The comparability of scales for job satisfaction," in W. E. Saris (ed.) *Variation in Response Function: A Source of Measurement Error* (pp. 178-199). Amsterdam, The Netherlands: Sociometric Research Foundation.

BELSON, W. A. (1981) *The Design and Understanding of Survey Questions.* London: Gower.

BEMELMANS-SPORK, M., and SIKKEL, D. (1985) "Observation of prices with hand-held computers." *Statistical Journal of the United Nations Economic Commission for Europe* 3(2). Geneva, Switzerland: United Nations Economic Commission for Europe.

88

BEMELMANS-SPORK, M., and SIKKEL, D. (1986) "Data collection with handheld computers." *Proceedings of the International Statistical Institute, 45th Session* (Vol. 3, Topic 18.3). Voorberg, The Netherlands: International Statistical Institute.

BILLIET, J., LOOSVELDT, G., and WATERPLAS, L. (1984) *Het Survey-Interview Onderzocht [The Survey Interview Evaluated]*. Leuven, Belgium: Department Sociologie.

BLAIR, E., and BURTON, S. (1986) "Processes used in the formulation of behavioral frequency reports in surveys," in *American Statistical Association Proceedings* (pp. 481-487). Alexandria, VA: American Statistical Association.

BOEREMA, E., BADEN, R. D., and BON, E. (1987) "Computer assisted face-to-face interviewing," in *ESOMAR Marketing Research Congress, 40th Session* (pp. 829-849). Amsterdam, The Netherlands: European Society for Opinion and Market Research.

BON, E. (1988) "Correction for variation in response behavior," in W. E. Saris (ed.) *Variation in Response Function: A Source of Measurement Error* (pp. 147-165). Amsterdam, The Netherlands: Sociometric Research Foundation.

BRADBURN, N. M., SUDMAN, S., BLAIR, E., and STOCKING, C. (1978) "Question threat and response bias." *Public Opinion Quarterly* 42: 221-234.

BRENNER, M. (1982) "Response effects of role-restricted characteristics of the interviewer," in W. Dijkstra and J. van der Zouwen (eds.) *Response Behaviour in the Survey Interview* (pp. 131-165). London: Academic Press.

BRUINSMA, C., SARIS, W. E., and GALLHOFER, I. N. (1980) "A study of systematic errors in survey research: The effect of the perception of other people's opinions," in C. P. Middendorp (ed.) *Proceedings of the Dutch Sociometric Society Congress* (pp. 117-135). Amsterdam, The Netherlands: Sociometric Research Foundation.

CARPENTER, E. H. (1988) "Software tools for data collection: Microcomputer-assisted interviewing." *Social Science Computer Review* 6: 353-368.

CLAYTON, R., and HARREL, L. J. (1989) "Developing a cost model for alternative data collection methods: Mail, CATI and TDE," in *American Statistical Association Proceedings* (pp. 264-269). Alexandria, VA: American Statistical Association.

CLEMENS, J. (1984) "The use of viewdata panels for data," in *Are Interviewers Obsolete? Drastic Changes in Data Collection and Data Presentation* (pp. 47-65). Amsterdam, The Netherlands: European Society for Opinion and Market Research.

CONNETT, W. E., BLACKBURN, Z., GEBLER, N., GREENWELL, M., HANSEN, S. E., and PRICE, P. (1990) *A Report on the Evaluation of Three CATI Systems.* Ann Arbor, MI: Survey Research Center.

CONVERSE, J. M., and PRESSER, S. (1986) *Survey Questions: Handcrafting the Standardized Questionnaire.* Beverly Hills, CA: Sage.

COUPER, M., and GROVES, R. (1989) *Interviewer Expectations Regarding CAPI: Results of Laboratory Tests II.* Washington, DC: Bureau of Labor Statistics.

COUPER, M., GROVES, R., and JACOBS, C. A. (1989) *Building Predictive Models of CAPI Acceptance in a Field Interviewing Staff.* Paper presented at the Annual Research Conference of the Bureau of the Census.

DANIELSSON, L., and MAARSTAD, P. A. (1982) *Statistical Data Collection with Hand-Held Computers: A Consumer Price Index.* Orebo, Sweden: Statistics Sweden.

de BIE, S. E., STOOP, I. A. L., and de VRIES, K. L. M. (1989) *CAI Software: An Evaluation of Software for Computer-Assisted Interviewing.* Amsterdam, The Netherlands: Stichting Interuniversitair Institut voor Sociaal Wetenschappelijk Onderzoek.

de PIJPER, W. M., and SARIS, W. E. (1986a) "Computer assisted interviewing using home computers." *European Research* 14: 144-152.

de PIJPER, W. M., and SARIS, W. E. (1986b) *The Formulation of Interviews Using the Program INTERV.* Amsterdam, The Netherlands: Sociometric Research Foundation.

DEKKER, F., and DORN, P. (1984) *Computer-Assisted Telephonic Interviewing: A Research Project in the Netherlands*. Paper presented at the Conference of the Institute of British Geographers, Durham, United Kingdom.

DIJKSTRA, W. (1983) *Beinvloeding van Antwoorden in Survey-Interviews [Influence on Answers in Survey Research]*. Unpublished doctoral dissertation, Vrije Univeristeit, Amsterdam, The Netherlands.

DIJKSTRA, W., and van der ZOUWEN, J. (eds.) (1982) *Response Behaviour in the Survey Interview*. London: Academic Press.

DUTKA, S., and FRANKEL, L. R. (1980) "Sequential survey design through the use of computer assisted telephone interviewing," in *American Statistical Association Proceedings* (pp. 73-76). Alexandria, VA: American Statistical Association.

FINK, J. C. (1983) "CATI's first decade: The Chilton experience." *Sociological Methods and Research* 12: 153-168.

GAVRILOV, A. J. (1988, November) *Computer Assisted Interviewing in the USSR.* Paper presented at the International Methodology Conference, Moscow.

GONZALEZ, M. E. (1990) *Computer Assisted Survey Information Collection* (Working Paper No. 19). Washington, DC: Statistical Policy Office.

GROVES, R. M. (1983) "Implications of CATI: Costs, errors, and organization of telephone survey research." *Sociological Methods and Research* 12: 199-215.

GROVES, R. M. (1989) *Survey Errors and Survey Costs*. New York: John Wiley.

GROVES, R. M., and NICHOLLS, W. L., II. (1986) "The status of computer-assisted telephone interviewing: Part II. Data quality issues." *Journal of Official Statistics* 2: 117-134.

HARTMAN, H., and SARIS, W. E. (1991, February) *Data Collection on Expenditures*. Paper presented at the Workshop on Diary Surveys, Stockholm, Sweden.

HOUSE, C. C. (1985) "Questionnaire design with computer assisted interviewing." *Journal of Official Statistics* 1: 209-219.

HOUSE, C. C., and NICHOLLS, W. L., II. (1988) "Questionnaire design for CATI: Design objectives and methods," in R. M. Groves, P. P. Biemer, L. E. Lyberg, J. T. Massey, W. L. Nicholls II, and J. Waksberg (eds.) *Telephone Survey Methodology* (pp. 421-437). New York: John Wiley.

JABINE, T. B. (1985) "A tool for developing and understanding survey questionnaires." *Journal of Official Statistics* 1: 189-207.

KALFS, N. (1986) *Het Construeren van Meetinstrumenten voor Quasi Collectieve Voorzieningen en Huishoudelijke Productie* [The Construction of Measurement Instruments for Quasi Collective Goods and Household Products] (Research Memorandum No. 861117). Amsterdam, The Netherlands: Sociometric Research Foundation.

KALTON, G., and SCHUMAN, H. (1982) "The effect of the question on survey response answers: A review." *Journal of the Royal Statistical Society* 145: 42-57.

KERSTEN, A. (1988) *Computer Gestuurd Interviewen [Computer Assisted Interviewing]*. Unpublished master's thesis, University of Amsterdam, The Netherlands.

KERSTEN, A., VERWEIJ, M., HARTMAN, H., and GALLHOFER, I. N. (1990) *Reduction of Measurement Errors by Computer Assisted Interviewing*. Amsterdam, The Netherlands: Sociometric Research Foundation.

KIESLER, S., and SPROULL, L. S. (1986) "Response effects in the electronic survey." *Public Opinion Quarterly* 50: 402-413.

KÖLTRINGER, R. (1991, April) *Design Effect in MTMM Studies*. Paper presented at the meeting of the International Research Group on Evaluation of Measurement Instruments, Ludwigshafen, Germany.

LODGE, M. (1981) *Magnitude Scaling*. Beverly Hills, CA: Sage.

90

LODGE, M., CROSS, D., TURSKY, B., and TANENHAUS, J. (1975) "The psychophysical scaling and validation of a political support scale." *American Journal of Political Science* 19: 611-649.

LOFTUS, E. F., and MARBURGER, W. (1983) "Since the eruption of Mt. St. Helen did anyone beat you up? Improving the accuracy of retrospective reports with landmark events." *Memory and Cognition* 11: 114-120.

LORD, F. M., and NOVICK, M. R. (1968) *Statistical Theories of Mental Test Scores.* London: Addison-Wesley.

MOLENAAR, N. J. (1986) *Formuleringseffecten in Survey-Interviews: Een Nonexperimenteel Onderzoek [Question Wording Effects in Survey Interviews]*. Amsterdam, The Netherlands: Vrije Univeristeit Uitgeverij.

NELSON, D. D. (1985) "Informal testing as a means of questionnaire development." *Journal of Official Statistics* 1: 179-188.

NETER, J., and WAKSBERG, J. (1963) "Effect of interviewing designated respondent in household surveys of home owner's expenditures on alterations and repairs." *Applied Statistics* 12: 46-60.

NETER, J., and WAKSBERG, J. (1964) "A study of response errors in expenditures data from household interviews." *Journal of American Statistical Association* 59: 18-55.

NETER, J., and WAKSBERG, J. (1965) *Response Errors in Collection of Expenditures Data by Household Interviews* (Technical Report No. 11J). Washington, DC: Bureau of the Census.

NICHOLLS, W. L., II. (1978) "Experiences with CATI in a large-scale survey." *American Statistical Association Proceedings* (pp. 9-17). Alexandria, VA: American Statistical Association.

NICHOLLS, W. L., II. (1988) "Computer-assisted telephone interviewing: A general introduction," in R. M. Groves, P. P. Biemer, L. E. Lyberg, J. T. Massey, W. L. Nicholls II, and J. Waksberg (eds.) *Telephone Survey Methodology* (pp. 377-387). New York: John Wiley.

NICHOLLS, W. L., II, and GROVES, R. M. (1986) "The status of computer-assisted telephone interviewing." *Journal of Official Statistics* 2: 93-115.

NICHOLLS, W. L., II, and HOUSE, C. C. (1987) "Designing questionnaires for computer assisted interviewing: A focus on program correctness," in *Proceedings of the Third Annual Research Conference of the U.S. Bureau of the Census* (pp. 95-111). Washington, DC: Government Printing Office.

PALIT, C., and SHARP, H. (1983) "Microcomputer-assisted telephone interviewing." *Sociological Methods and Research* 12: 169-191.

PHILLIPS, D. L., and CLANCY, K. J. (1970) "Response bias in field studies of mental illness." *American Sociological Review* 35: 503-515.

PULSE TRAIN TECHNOLOGY. (1984) *Limited Questionnaire Specification Language.* Esher, United Kingdom: Author.

SARIS, W. E. (1982) "Different questions, different variables," in C. Fornell (ed.) *Second Generation of Multivariate Analysis* (pp. 78-96). New York: Praeger.

SARIS, W. E. (1988) *Variation in Response Functions: A Source of Measurement Error.* Amsterdam, The Netherlands: Sociometric Research Foundation.

SARIS, W. E. (1989) "A technological revolution in data collection." *Quality and Quantity* 23: 333-348.

SARIS, W. E., and ANDREWS, F. M. (in press) "Evaluation of measurement instruments using a structural modeling approach," in P. P. Biemer, R. M. Groves, L. E. Lyberg, N. Mathiowetz, and S. Sudman (eds.) *Measurement Errors in Surveys.* New York: John Wiley.

SARIS, W. E., de PIJPER, W. M., and NEIJENS, P. (1982) "Some notes on the computer steered interview," in C. Middendorp (eds.) *Proceedings of the Sociometry Meeting* (pp. 306-310). Amsterdam, The Netherlands: Sociometric Research Foundation.

SARIS, W. E., and de ROOY, K. (1988) "What kinds of terms should be used for reference points?" in W. E. Saris (ed.) *Variation in Response Functions: A Source of Measurement Error in Attitude Research* (pp. 199-219). Amsterdam, The Netherlands: Sociometric Research Foundation.

SARIS, W. E., van de PUTTE, B., MAAS, K., and SEIP, H. (1988) "Variation in response function: Observed and created," in W. E. Saris (ed.) *Variation in Response Function: A Source of Measurement Error* (pp. 165-178). Amsterdam, The Netherlands: Sociometric Research Foundation.

SCHUMAN, H., and PRESSER, S. (1981) *Questions and Answers in Attitude Surveys: Experiments on Question Form Wording and Context.* London: Academic Press.

SHANKS, J. M. (1989) "Information technology and survey research: Where do we go from here?" *Journal of Official Statistics* 5: 3-21.

SIKKEL, D. (1985) "Models for memory effects." *Journal of the American Statistical Association* 80: 835-841.

SILBERSTEIN, A. R. (1989) "Recall effects in the U.S. consumer expenditure interview survey." *Journal of Official Statistics* 5: 125-142.

SOCIOMETRIC RESEARCH FOUNDATION. (1988, Spring) "New facilities of INTERV for panel research." *SRF Newsletter.*

SPAETH, M. A. (1990) "CATI facilities at academic research organizations." *Survey Research* 2(2): 11-14.

STEVENS, S. S. (1975) *Psychophysics: Introduction to Its Perceptual Neural and Social Prospects.* New York: John Wiley.

SUDMAN, S., and BRADBURN, N. M. (1973) "Effects of time and memory factors on responses in surveys." *Journal of the American Statistical Association* 68: 805-815.

SUDMAN, S., and BRADBURN, N. M. (1974) *Response Effects in Surveys.* Hawthorne, NY: Aldine.

THORNBERRY, O., ROWE, B., and BIGGER, R. (1990, June) *Use of CAPI with the U.S. National Health Interview Survey.* Paper presented at the meeting of the International Sociological Association, Madrid, Spain.

THORNTON, A., FREEDMAN, D. S., and CAMBURN, D. (1982) "Obtaining respondent cooperation in family panel studies." *Sociological Methods and Research* 11: 33-51.

TORTORA, R. (1985) "CATI in agricultural statistical agency." *Journal of Official Statistics* 1: 301-314.

van BASTELAER, A., KERSSEMAKERS, F., and SIKKEL, D. (1988) "A test of the Netherlands continuous labour force survey with hand held computers: Interviewer behaviour and data quality," in D. Sikkel (ed.) *Quality Aspects of Statistical Data Collection* (pp. 67-92). Amsterdam, The Netherlands: Sociometric Research Foundation.

van DOORN, L. (1987-1988) "Het gebruik van microcomputers in panelonderzoek" ["The use of microcomputers in panel research"], in *Jaarboek van de Nederlandse Vereniging Voor Marktonderzoekers* (pp. 7-23).

van DOORN, L., SARIS, W. E., and LODGE, M. (1983) "Discrete or continuous measurement: What difference does it make?" *Kwantitatieve Methoden* 10: 104-120.

VERWEIJ, M. J., KALFS, N. J., and SARIS, W. E. (1986) *Tijdsbestedings-Onderzoek Middels: Tele-Interviewing en de Mogelijkheden Voor Segmentatie [Time-Budget Research Using Tele-Interviewing and the Possibilities for Segmentation]* (Research Memo No. 87031). Amsterdam, The Netherlands: Sociometric Research Foundation.

WEBB, E., CAMPBELL, D. T., SCHWARTZ, R. D., and SECHREST, L. (1981) *Unobtrusive Measures: Nonreactive Research in the Social Sciences.* Boston: Houghton Mifflin.

WEEKS, M. F. (1988) "Call scheduling with CATI: Current capabilities and methods," in R. M. Groves, P. P. Biemer, L. E. Lyberg, J. T. Massey, W. L. Nicholls II, and J. Waksberg (eds.) *Telephone Survey Methodology* (pp. 403-421). New York: John Wiley.

WEGENER, B. (1982) *Social Attitudes and Psychophysical Measurement.* Hillsdale, NJ: Lawrence Earlbaum.

WILLENBORG, L. C. R. J. (1989) *Computational Aspects of Survey Data Processing.* Amsterdam, The Netherlands: CWI.

WINTER, D. L. S., and CLAYTON, R. L. (1990) *Speech Data Entry: Results of the First Test of Voice Recognition for Data Collection.* Washington, DC: Bureau of Labor Statistics.

ABOUT THE AUTHOR

WILLEM E. SARIS is professor in the department of Methods and Techniques for Political Science at the University of Amsterdam, The Netherlands. He received his masters in sociology at the University of Utrecht and his Ph.D. in social science at the University of Amsterdam. He is currently Chairman of the Sociometric Research Foundation. He has published numerous professional articles and books. Some of his present research interests involve: Structural equation modeling, improvement of measurement in social science research, and the development of computer-assisted interviewing.